HOW TO WIN
IN SMALL
CLAIMS COURT
IN FLORIDA

Seventh Edition

Mark Warda
Attorney at Law

SPHINX® PUBLISHING
AN IMPRINT OF SOURCEBOOKS, INC.®
NAPERVILLE, ILLINOIS
www.SphinxLegal.com

Seventh Edition, 2002

Published by: **Sourcebooks, Inc.**

Naperville Office
P.O. Box 4410
Naperville, Illinois 60567-4410
630-961-3900
Fax: 630-961-2168
www.sourcebooks.com
wwwSphinxLegal.com

This publication is designed to provide accurate and authoritative information in regard to the subject matter covered. It is sold with the understanding that the publisher is not engaged in rendering legal, accounting, or other professional service. If legal advice or other expert assistance is required, the services of a competent professional person should be sought.

From a Declaration of Principles Jointly Adopted by a Committee of the
American Bar Association and a Committee of Publishers and Associations

This product is not a substitute for legal advice.

Disclaimer required by Texas statutes.

Library of Congress Cataloging-in-Publication Data
Warda, Mark.
  How to win in small claims court in Florida / Mark Warda.-- 7th ed.
      p. cm. -- (Legal survival guides)
Includes index.
  ISBN 1-57248-204-4 (alk. paper)
  1. Small claims courts--Florida--Popular works. I. Title. II. Series.

KFF521.Z9 W37 2002
347.759'04--dc21

                                        2002072401

Printed and bound in the United States of America.
VHG Paperback — 10 9 8 7 6 5 4 3 2 1

Contents

Using Self-Help Law Books

Before using a self-help law book, you should realize the advantages and disadvantages of doing your own legal work and understand the challenges and diligence that this requires.

THE GROWING TREND

Rest assured that you won't be the first or only person handling your own legal matter. For example, in some states, more than seventy-five percent of divorces and other cases have at least one party representing him or herself. Because of the high cost of legal services, this is a major trend and many courts are struggling to make it easier for people to represent themselves. However, some courts are not happy with people who do not use attorneys and refuse to help them in any way. For some, the attitude is, "Go to the law library and figure it out for yourself."

We at Sphinx write and publish self-help law books to give people an alternative to the often complicated and confusing legal books found in most law libraries. We have made the explanations of the law as simple and easy to understand as possible. Of course, unlike an attorney advising an individual client, we cannot cover every conceivable possibility.

COST/VALUE ANALYSIS

Whenever you shop for a product or service, you are faced with various levels of quality and price. In deciding what product or service to buy, you make a cost/value analysis on the basis of your willingness to pay and the quality you desire.

When buying a car, you decide whether you want transportation, comfort, status, or sex appeal. Accordingly, you decide among such choices as a Neon, a Lincoln, a Rolls Royce, or a Porsche. Before making a decision, you usually weigh the merits of each option against the cost.

When you get a headache, you can take a pain reliever (such as aspirin) or visit a medical specialist for a neurological examination. Given this choice, most people, of course, take a pain reliever, since it costs only pennies; whereas a medical examination costs hundreds of dollars and takes a lot of time. This is usually a logical choice because it is rare to need anything more than a pain reliever for a headache. But in some cases, a headache may indicate a brain tumor and failing to see a specialist right away can result in complications. Should everyone with a headache go to a specialist? Of course not, but people treating their own illnesses must realize that they are betting on the basis of their cost/value analysis of the situation. They are taking the most logical option.

The same cost/value analysis must be made when deciding to do one's own legal work. Many legal situations are very straight forward, requiring a simple form and no complicated analysis. Anyone with a little intelligence and a book of instructions can handle the matter without outside help.

But there is always the chance that complications are involved that only an attorney would notice. To simplify the law into a book like this, several legal cases often must be condensed into a single sentence or paragraph. Otherwise, the book would be several hundred pages long and too complicated for most people. However, this simplification necessarily leaves out many details and nuances that would apply to special or unusual situations. Also, there are many ways to interpret most legal questions. Your case may come before a judge who disagrees with the analysis of our authors.

Therefore, in deciding to use a self-help law book and to do your own legal work, you must realize that you are making a cost/value analysis. You have decided that the money you will save in doing it yourself outweighs the chance that your case will not turn out to your satisfaction. Most people handling their own simple legal matters never have a problem, but occasionally people find that it ended up costing them more to have an attorney straighten out the situation than it would have if they had hired an attorney in the beginning. Keep this in mind if you decide to handle your own case, and be sure to consult an attorney if you feel you might need further guidance.

LOCAL RULES

The next thing to remember is that a book that covers the law for the entire nation, or even for an entire state, cannot possibly include every procedural difference of every county court. Whenever possible, we provide the exact form needed; however, in some areas, each county, or even each judge, may require unique forms and procedures. In our *state* books, our forms usually cover the majority of counties in the state, or provide examples of the type of form that will be required. In our *national* books, our forms are sometimes even more general in nature but are designed to give a good idea of the type of form that will be needed in most locations. Nonetheless, keep in mind that your *state*, county, or judge may have a requirement, or use a form, that is not included in this book.

You should not necessarily expect to be able to get all of the information and resources you need solely from within the pages of this book. This book will serve as your guide, giving you specific information whenever possible and helping you to find out what else you will need to know. This is just like if you decided to build your own backyard deck. You might purchase a book on how to build decks. However, such a book would not include the building codes and permit requirements of every city, town, county, and township in the nation; nor would it include the lumber, nails, saws, hammers, and other materials and tools you would need to actually build the deck. You would use the book as your guide, and then do some work and research involving such matters as whether you need a permit of some kind, what type and grade of wood are available in your area, whether to use hand tools or power tools, and how to use those tools.

Before using the forms in a book like this, you should check with your court clerk to see if there are any local rules of which you should be aware, or local forms you will need to use. Often, such forms will require the same information as the forms in the book but are merely laid out differently, use slightly different language, or use different color paper so the clerks can easily find them. They will sometimes require additional information.

CHANGES IN
THE LAW

Besides being subject to state and local rules and practices, the law is subject to change at any time. The courts and the legislatures of all fifty states are constantly revising the laws. It is possible that while you are reading this book, some aspect of the law is being changed or a court is interpreting a law in a different way. You should always check the most recent statutes, rules and regulations to see what, if any changes have been made.

In most cases, the change will be of minimal significance. A form will be redesigned, additional information will be required, or a waiting period will be extended. As a result, you might need to revise a form, file an extra form, or wait out a longer time period; these types of changes will not usually affect the outcome of your case. On the other hand, sometimes a major part of the law is changed, the entire law in a particular area is rewritten, or a case that was the basis of a central legal point is overruled. In such instances, your entire ability to pursue your case may be impaired.

Again, you should weigh the value of your case against the cost of an attorney and make a decision as to what you believe is in your best interest.

Introduction

Florida's small claims court system provides a useful procedure for collecting small debts. Many claims are too small to warrant the services of an attorney, but too big to ignore. Chapter 1 will give you a small claims overview.

Simply filing a small claims case often gets results from people who know they owe money but have not gotten around to paying it. Being brought before a judge is not something people look forward to, and sometimes delivery of a summons brings an immediate check. On the other hand, going through the whole case and winning a judgment may be useless. If a person has no money, there is nothing for you to collect. Chapter 2 will give you some considerations to think about before you sue.

In recent years, the small claims rules were changed for better and for worse. They are better because they now allow claims of up to $5,000 to be filed. They are worse in that they attempt to stop judges from telling parties what the law is unless represented by an attorney.

The purpose of the second change was to stop judges from helping one side of a case when the other was represented by an attorney. But they went much further. The previous rule allowed judges to assist parties on procedure to be followed, presentation of material evidence and questions of law. Now the judges are only supposed to assist in "court-room decorum" and "order of presentation of evidence," and the rule specifically provides that "the court may not instruct any party not represented by an attorney on accepted rules of law." See Florida Small Claims Rule 7.140 in Appendix B.

It is unclear just what effect this will have on parties' rights or how the judges will interpret the rule. It is hard to imagine that a judge could run a courtroom without explaining to the parties what the law requires of them. One judge told the author that some judges are liberally interpreting the rule to allow them to at least tell the parties what the court will be looking for.

In some states the judges are specifically allowed to instruct both parties of what their legal rights are and in others lawyers are not even allowed in small claims court. But in Florida the lawyers have a stronger say in the rules of court. In fact they draft them for the court to approve. Sometimes the court goes further than the attorneys want in helping the public, but not always.

In any case the new rule should make the parties do more legal research before filing a case. Be sure you know the legal basis for your type of claim and that you have the necessary proof. Read Chapter 3 for this information.

This book provides the basics. For further guidance on the specific facts of your case you can do some research at the law library or consult with an attorney. While it may not be cost effective to hire an attorney for your entire case it is often well worth getting some guidance from one before filing. If the other side has an attorney you really should get a legal opinion of your side of the case and advice as to what evidence and arguments will be important in court.

If you do not know an attorney you can find one through the Florida Bar lawyer referral services. The numbers are found in Appendix A.

Before filing your case, it is advisable to read this entire text. Sometimes information relating to the end of the process is important in planning the beginning, or a decision made in the beginning may affect the procedures in the end. While Chapter 4 will give you some defenses, Chapter 5 explains countersuing. These are two items you should know about in the beginning so you can plan your strategy.

Chapters 6 through 8 will get you through procedure and rules. Chapter 9 will explain appeals.

Don't forget to use the handy checklists in Appendix C so you don't miss any steps. For your convenience, Appendix D has many forms ready for your use.

SMALL CLAIMS COURT, GENERALLY

1

Small claims court is a forum in which people with differences can have a judge decide their legal rights. The parties do not need to be represented by a lawyer, and the rules of procedure are simplified so that the technical rules usually used in court are not necessary.

Persons winning a case in small claims court are granted a *judgment*. This is a court order stating that they are entitled to something such as a sum of money or the return of some piece of property. In some cases the judgment is not worth anything, for example when the other person has no money with which to pay it. But with persistence money can often be collected on a judgment. A judgment can be good for twenty years as a lien on any property owned by the person it is made against. (See Chapter 8, "Collecting Your Judgment".)

TYPES OF CASES THAT CAN BE HEARD

Small claims court is usually used to collect small sums of money or to obtain the return of property. Recently the law was changed to allow small claims court judges to hear equitable actions. (Florida Statutes (Fla. Stat.), Section (Sec.) 34.01(4).) These are cases in which the court is asked to determine legal rights or to command someone to do something. Some examples of equitable remedies are recision of a deal which was grossly unfair, restitution when a party needs to be restored to an original position, reformation of a contract to comply with the original intent of the parties, and specific performance when property is one-of-a-kind and one party refuses to sell.

HOW MUCH YOU CAN SUE FOR

A few years ago, the limit in small claims court was raised from $2500 to $5000.

If your claim is for more than the limit of small claims court you may still use small claims court if you are willing to accept an amount up to the limit.

Example: If someone owes you $5500 and the limit is $5000, you may want to sue in small claims court and be happy with a judgment for $5000. This would be better than hiring a lawyer to sue for the whole $5500 in county court since his or her fees would probably be more than the $500 you would have to forego in small claims court. If you do agree to accept the $5000 limit in small claims court, you must realize that you have given up your right to the higher amount.

If you sue for a debt greater than the limit, the defendant may ask that your case be thrown out because it exceeds the limit. Therefore, you should make clear in your court papers or to the judge at the hearing that you wish to waive all amounts over the limit.

Another possibility is to divide your claim into several suits, each of which is under the limit.

Example: If you loaned someone $4000 on two different occasions, you could probably treat each loan as a separate transaction and file two suits for $4000 each. However, if you gave him one check for $8000 you could probably not break it into two suits just to get into small claims court. The person you are suing may try to have the suits combined in order to lower the amount of the possible judgment, so you should be prepared to explain to the judge why the matters are separate transactions.

One way to make it less obvious that your claims may be related is to file them on different dates. This way you will have different hearings possibly before different judges.

In addition to the amount of your claim, you will be allowed to collect your filing fee and service of process fee and possibly other costs of bringing your suit.

PROCEDURE

The small claims court uses a two-hearing procedure. After a **STATEMENT OF CLAIM** is filed with the clerk of the court, a date is set for a pretrial conference. The purpose of the pretrial conference is to:

- simplify the issues;
- decide if pleadings need to be amended;
- see what matters are admitted to be true;
- decide which witnesses are necessary;
- see if settlement is possible; and,
- cover any other matters that the court thinks are important.

You do not have to bring any evidence or witnesses to this conference. Under the rules, the pretrial conference should be set no more than thirty-five days from the date of filing the case.

It is important to appear in person at this hearing or you will automatically lose. (If you plan to be represented by an attorney, he or she can appear in your place.) If you cannot make it to the pretrial conference for some important reason, call the court clerk and see if you can reschedule it, explaining your reason. If you have already missed your hearing and had a judgment entered against you, see Chapter 9, "Appeals and Re-Hearings." At the pretrial conference a trial date is set.

At the pretrial conference the judge may also explain to you what witnesses or evidence will be important and may instruct you to give a list of your evidence or witnesses to the other side prior to the trial. The court might also hear any motions of the parties, such as motions for continuance or to dismiss. However, most people who come to court without attorneys do not use motions.

When the judge sets the trial date you should be sure that you and your witnesses will be available on that date. If you come unprepared for trial and do not have a valid legal reason for not being prepared, the case will be decided anyway, and you will not have a second chance to present your side.

NEEDING AN ATTORNEY

Small claims court was originally designed to let people represent themselves without the expense of hiring an attorney. However, the rules were changed and judges no longer can explain the law to the parties. The parties must know the law and present the right evidence or they will lose.

If your case is simple and you take the time to do some research, you probably do not need an attorney. But if the issues are complicated, you should at least consult with an attorney for advice in handling your case. Some attorneys will provide advice at an hourly rate without actually handling the case in court. Small Claims Rule 7.140(f) allows attorneys to represent a party over the phone without appearing in court (if the judge permits).

Any time the other side hires an attorney you should consult one too. A new rule forbids judges from explaining the law to unrepresented parties, so you may be easy prey to a lawyer who finds a fatal flaw in your case. For a list of lawyer referral services, see Appendix A.

A rule adopted in 1988 allows a party who has won a case and is not represented by an attorney to have a hearing before a judge to discover a defendant's assets. (Small Claims Rule 7.221.) This is a distinct advantage because it is much cheaper than having an attorney conduct a deposition in aid of execution. (see Chapter 8.)

In most cases, each party must pay his or her own attorney's fees, no matter who wins. But in some cases, such as where a written contract allows attorney's fees, or in landlord/tenant cases, the loser must pay the winner's attorney's fees. If yours is such a case, then it is important to get the advice of an attorney before filing your case, especially if the other side is expected to have an attorney. Otherwise, a simple mistake on your part may result in the other side winning the case plus attorney's fees.

If you merely consult an attorney on your case, you may or may not be able to get the other side to pay the fees. The other side will probably argue that since the attorney did not appear in court you are not entitled to fees, but you should argue that you did consult an attorney concerning the case and kept the fees down by not having the lawyer spend unnecessary time in court. Be sure to have a bill from the lawyer to present to the judge.

If you expect to use an attorney, you should add an additional paragraph as the last claim in your complaint as follows:

```
Plaintiff has retained an attorney and is oblig-
ated to pay a reasonable fee for his (her)
services.
```

NOTE: *If you do not ask for attorney fees in your claim you might not get them.*

WHERE YOU CAN GET HELP

The court clerks are supposed to help you prepare the papers filed in your case. They can usually be very helpful in avoiding costly mistakes. The judge at the pretrial conference may tell the parties what evidence will be necessary to win the case, or may pass out an instruction sheet explaining what type of evidence is necessary.

You should always listen carefully to the advice of the clerk and the judge. If they say something is important in your case, don't assume you have a better idea. Listen to the people who run the show. They will decide who wins the case.

If the judge at the pretrial conference says that you will need a certain piece of evidence to win the case, such as an original document or certain physical evidence, and you know it will be impossible to get, mention this to the judge and explain the situation. If that evidence is impossible to obtain, the judge may suggest substitute evidence which will be acceptable.

If the judge tells you that you will need a certain witness, you will probably lose if you cannot get that witness to come to court. If the person is an expert, such as a mechanic, you may have to pay his hourly fee to take time off work to appear for you. If the person is a witness to the incident you are suing over, you may have to have the clerk issue a subpoena ordering them to appear. The rules now allow a witness to appear by telephone. If necessary, ask the judge if this may be arranged in your case.

NOTE: *The biggest mistake people make in small claims court is failing to follow the instructions of what evidence will be needed.*

The rules that small claims court follow are contained in Appendix B of this book. If you have any questions about how a procedure works, you should check these rules.

If you are serious about your case and would like to do further research into formal rules of procedure, you should consult a book on Florida civil procedure. While small claims court has its own rules, many legal principles such as who may be sued are in the books about regular civil procedure. The best book on Florida civil procedure is *Trawick's Florida Practice and Procedure,* by Henry Trawick.

WHAT YOU CAN RECOVER

As a general rule, you can only recover actual out-of-pocket losses directly relating to the subject matter of the suit.

Example: If you are suing a cleaners for ruining a dress or an auto mechanic for improperly repairing your car, you can sue for the value of the dress or for the cost of proper repairs.

You cannot recover for the fact that you missed a job interview or a party because you didn't have the dress or car. Nor can you recover lost wages for time you spend in court or your travel costs to court, even if you had to fly in from out-of-state.

In a personal injury case there may be more damages related to the accident. For example, in a car accident you may have medical bills, lost pay from missing work, damage to your car, and pain and suffering.

If you are the *prevailing party*, meaning you won on a significant issue in the case, then you may be awarded your costs of the suit. These include your filing fee, sheriff's fee and witness fees. Therefore, if you have a good case, it might be worth spending $100 in costs to win a $50 case because you would be entitled to $150 if you win.

As discussed in the next chapter, you should ask for as much as possible within the small claims court limit in order to improve your negotiating position (even if you know you will not be granted everything in court). As a practical matter, you usually will not get much more than out-of-pocket losses.

TERMINOLOGY

There are many terms used in small claims court and they should be understood by all the parties. There is a glossary after Chapter 9 that has many of these terms defined.

BEFORE YOU SUE 2

Before you file a case in any court you should first analyze whether it is worth your time and effort to go through the whole process. You want to file a case because you are upset about something, but it will be even more upsetting if you lose—especially if you end up paying damages to the other side. Most cases settle out of court because you can never predict what result you will get in court. No matter how right you are, or how strong your case is, the court can rule the other way for any number of reasons.

DECIDING IF YOU HAVE A CASE

In order to win a lawsuit against someone, you must be able to prove they are liable under some acceptable legal theory. In many instances, a person who has clearly suffered a loss may not be able to win their case because the law does not place the liability on another person. Before filing your case you must find a legal theory that will allow you to collect. Some cases are easy. If a person did something intentionally (like break your window) or failed to do something that was legally required (like pay back a loan) then you have a clear case.

But in other cases you must use a more complicated theory, such as *negligence* or *implied warranty*. In cases like these you will only win if the facts of your case fit into the legal definitions of negligence or implied warranty.

Example 1: If you are struck by lightning while walking at Disney World, the owners will probably not be liable because the courts consider lightning an "act of God" and not the legal responsibility of the landowner. (A person once tried to sue God for an act of God. He served the papers on a local church as an "agent of God." But the court said that the church was not legally able to accept service of process for God so the court "did not have jurisdiction over the defendant.")

Example 2: Imagine you have rented a house from a landlord. When you signed the lease you agreed to take care of minor maintenance and the landlord agreed to charge you less rent. Now suppose you fixed a board on the steps and later it broke and you fell, breaking your leg. Even though the landlord owns the property and has insurance against liability, he will probably not have to pay for your broken leg because you had the duty to maintain the premises and you are the one who improperly fixed the step which broke.

If you signed a contract or received any papers from the other party relating to the transaction, you should read them before filing suit. Sometimes they will limit your legal rights or your right to bring suit. If a business made promises about a product but the contract said the product was sold "as is" and that "oral representations cannot be relied upon," you may be out of luck. Or if your contract with your stock broker says that you agree to arbitration, you may have given up your right to sue.

In some cases, the papers used by the party may not have any legal effect. A lease may say that a landlord is not liable for injuries on the premises, but in some instances Florida law states otherwise and this overrules the wording of the lease. A ticket you receive when bringing an item for repair may say that the repair shop is not liable if the item is lost or destroyed, but Florida law may allow you to recover anyway.

If you have any doubts about your rights you should check with an attorney or do some legal research yourself. Many types of claims are explained in this book, but if you are industrious you may want to do some extra legal research to find other grounds for your suit. You can do legal research at the law library found in most county courthouses or in many law schools. There are also several books on the market explaining how to do legal research.

PROVING YOUR CASE

Even if you have a good case, you will not win if you do not have enough proof to convince the judge that you are right. If all you have is a verbal agreement, it will be your word against the defendant's and the judge will have to decide who is more believable. If you do not have any evidence and the other side has evidence that supports his side of the case, you will be less likely to win.

Be sure to read the rules of evidence in Chapter 7. Also, ask your friends what they see as the best points of the other side's case. As a participant in the situation, you will not be able to effectively judge the other side's arguments. Your friends may provide an objective opinion. If there is a chance you will be *countersued*, you should consider consulting with an attorney. He or she may be able to point out a legal rule or other reason that you could lose the case.

DECIDING ON TIME AND EFFORT

Even if you have a legal claim, not all claims are worth bringing to court. Sometimes it may cost you more to take off work for two hearings than the claim is worth. If there is a chance you will be countersued then you are risking more than just your time and effort.

Of course, in many cases the principle is more important than the money and you may enjoy the process of getting justice from someone who took advantage of you. But be sure to consider what the case will involve before you start it.

You should also consider that it might not be worth the time and effort for the other side to fight your case. If the amount involved is small and they will have to take off work or hire an attorney, they may just settle with you without a trial. So merely filing your case may get results.

COLLECTING IF YOU WIN

If the person you want to sue has no money, it may be a waste of time to go to court. You cannot garnish the wages of the head of a family in Florida. Also, in Florida a large amount of a debtor's property is exempt from creditors' claims. So a judgment you spent time and court costs to obtain, may end up being a worthless piece of paper.

The best party to sue is a large corporation or a person with a lot of real estate or other assets. (You can check the property records in the courthouse and the state motor vehicle records to see what a person owns.) If you have a valid claim, a large corporation will probably pay you rather than spend the money to defend itself. If you are suing a person who owns real estate, your judgment can be placed as a lien on all of their holdings for up to twenty years.

The worst parties to sue are small corporations with no assets or people who have no assets and are supporting a family.

If you are not sure if the party is worth suing, you might want to read Chapter 8 in this book before fling your claim. It explains how to find out what a person's assets are.

> ***Warning***: You should not sue anyone unless you have a valid claim. If you file a suit and the judge decides there is really no legal or factual merit to it, he or she may place a judgment against you for all of the other party's attorney's fees and court costs.

STEPS BEFORE FILING SUIT

Before filing your suit you should attempt to work it out with the other person. People sometimes come to court and say they have not paid an amount owed because they were never asked. Even if you have asked the person to settle the matter, you should send at least one letter and keep a copy of it. This can be used as evidence in court that you have tried to resolve the matter.

In some counties there are *mediation* or *arbitration* services. If you think it might help, you should contact them before filing your suit and see if they can help you work something out with the other party.

When negotiating to settle a case you should be sure not to let the time limit pass for filing your case. There is a law called the *statute of limitations* which gives time limits as to when each type of suit can be filed. Once the deadline has passed, the claim is forever barred and may not be sued upon. For example, for a suit for professional malpractice the limit is two years, but for a suit on a promissory note the limit is five years. For other types of suits see Chapter 3.

If the limitations deadline is near and the person you are negotiating with seems to be delaying, you may have to file your suit to avoid missing the deadline. One way to avoid the deadline without filing suit is to have the person sign a *promissory note*. This is considered a new agreement and the limitation period begins five years from the date the final payment is due.

FILING YOUR CASE 3

In order to win your case you need to follow all the legal rules in preparing your papers. These include rules regarding who can sue and be sued, where to file, and what kinds of claims can be filed.

THOSE WHO CAN SUE

Any individual, corporation, partnership or other legal entity may use small claims court. In filing the suit, the party suing must be correctly identified. For some parties there are special rules.

CORPORATIONS

A corporation must be represented at all proceedings by a corporate officer or by an "employee authorized by an officer" of the corporation. Some counties require the employee to have a notarized statement signed by an officer giving them authority. Form 44, AUTHORIZATION TO REPRESENT CORPORATION, in this book can be used for this purpose. (see form 44, p.152.)

NONRESIDENTS

Nonresidents of Florida may sue in small claims court, but they may be required to post a *cost bond* of $100. (Fla. Stat., Sec. 57.011.) A cost bond is a guarantee by an insurance company to pay the costs of the defendant if he or she wins.

FICTITIOUS NAMES

A person using a *fictitious name* (a business name that is not one's legal name) must have registered the name with the Secretary of State or the case may be abated. (see page 18.) A person using a fictitious name must file the suit in his or her own name along with the fictitious name. For example, "John Smith, d/b/a The Gardening Center."

TRUSTEES AND
FIDUCIARIES

Trustees and *fiduciaries,* such as personal representatives of estates or guardians, may sue as long as they properly identify their role.

MINORS AND
INCOMPETENTS

Minors and *incompetents* (people for whom a guardian has been appointed due to lack of mental capacity) must sue through their guardian or parent. A parent is considered the natural guardian of a child and may sue without special permission. However, a person who is not a natural parent can only act for a child if he or she is appointed guardian by a court.

MULTIPLE
PARTIES

Although claims by multiple parties for money would probably exceed the small claims limit, several parties might want to get together to sue for other remedies.

Example: If someone is causing a nuisance in the neighborhood, several neighbors could file one suit (paying only one filing fee) to seek an end to the nuisance.

THOSE WHO CAN BE SUED

It is important to sue the correct party or your judgment may be worthless. Even worse, you may have to pay for a person's attorney's fee if you sue him or her without good legal grounds.

INDIVIDUALS

Be sure to get the exact name of the party you are suing. Do not sue "Mr. & Mrs. Smith." You need to have the correct spelling of their full names. If you don't know their middle names it is not crucial, but the more precise you are the better.

SPOUSES

Whenever you have legal grounds, you should sue both spouses. If you get a judgment against just one person and he or she owns property with a spouse, you may not be able to put a lien on it or seize it. But a judgment against both a husband and wife can be filed as a lien against all of the property owned by either or both of them. Whenever you have a plausible legal reason to sue a spouse, do it.

Example: If you are trying to collect back rent from a tenant, even if only one party usually paid the rent, you could argue that both were tenants and one was the agent of the other.

MINORS AND INCOMPETENTS
You cannot sue a person under eighteen years of age or an incompetent person unless you also sue his guardian or have one appointed by the court. For an injury caused by a minor, you could in most cases sue his natural parents. Having a guardian appointed by the court would require the services of an attorney.

CORPORATIONS
If you sue a corporation you must have the correct name of the corporation and you should serve the *registered agent*. You can get this information from the Secretary of State. The number is 850-488-9000 and the mailing address is:

> Division of Corporations
> P. O. Box 6327
> Tallahassee, FL 32314

You can also access corporate records on the internet. The site is:

> http://www.dos.state.fl.us/doc/corp_dir.html

A corporation with assets is a good target, but a *shell* corporation with no assets is not. It can be dissolved, making your claim worthless. An individual may have no assets or may file bankruptcy, but it is not as likely or as easy as dissolving a shell corporation. A new corporation can always be started, but an individual is stuck with his credit record for years.

In such a case, it is better if you can sue some of the individuals in the corporation. This can be done if the individuals signed documents without their corporate titles; or if the company name was used without the words "Inc.," "Corp." or "Co." after it; or if the individuals committed some sort of fraud. It can also be done where a corporation has been undercapitalized and in a few other circumstances.

Ignoring a corporate entity and suing the individuals behind it is called *piercing the corporate veil* and much has been written about it in legal books and periodicals. If you think you will need to pierce a corporate veil to win your case, you should research the subject further in your nearest law library.

PARTNERSHIPS

You cannot sue a partnership as such. You must sue the individuals who are the partners. If you do not know who the partners are, you should read the following section on fictitious names. For a limited partnership you need only sue the general partners. However, your judgment will only be against assets of the partnership and the general partners. The personal assets of the limited partners are not subject to claims against the partnership.

FICTITIOUS
NAMES

You cannot sue a "company" unless it is a corporation. If it is a sole proprietorship or a partnership, you must name the individuals and add "d/b/a" (doing business as) and then the company name. For example you might sue:

```
John Smith d/b/a Smith Company, or

John Smith, Raymond Smith and William Smith d/b/a
Smith Enterprises, a partnership
```

If you do not know who the principals of the business are, you can look them up. Prior to 1991, all business were supposed to register with the county if they were using a *fictitious name*. During 1991 and 1992, there was a transition to registration with the Secretary of State. However, not all businesses re-registered their names properly. Therefore, you should check both places to find the principles of the business. In your county the records are in the Official Records Office. The Secretary of State's address, phone number and web site is on the previous page.

If they have not registered, you can try the cross-reference telephone directory, or check the occupational license department of the city or county in which they are located. You could also try calling the company anonymously and asking for the owner's name. You might want to call the state attorney and report the company for not registering its name. It is a misdemeanor.

You can also access fictitious name records on the Internet at the site on page 17.

WHERE TO FILE YOUR SUIT

Unless you sue in the proper court, your case can be dismissed. The geographic area under the jurisdiction of a court is called its *venue*. The proper venue for a case can be any of the following:

- where the contract was entered into;

- where the event giving rise to the suit occurred;

- if the suit is to recover property or foreclose a lien, where the property involved is located;

- if an unsecured promissory note, where the note was signed or where the maker (signer) of the note resides;

- where any one of the defendants reside;

- any location agreed to in a contract; or,

- in an action for money due, if there is no agreement as to where a suit may be filed, then in the county where payment is to be made.

NOTE: *When the parties live in different counties, the proper place to sue is where the defendant lives unless one of the above exceptions applies. But if there are several defendants, you can pick which county to sue in because the county of any one defendant would be proper.*

In some counties that have more than one courthouse local rules require that suit be filed in one of the courthouses. Check with the clerk of small claims court to see if there is such a rule that applies to your case.

FEES

Officially, the filing fees are the same throughout the state, but many counties have other fees added on. Usually the fees will be in the following range:

Claims under $100	$10 to $80
Claims of $100 to $5000	$50 to $100

For *replevin* actions (a suit for return of property) there may be an additional fee of $47 or more.

In counties where the filing fee for a claim of $50 is $40 (plus the sheriff's fee), it may seem like a waste of time and money to sue. But keep in mind that if you win the other party will have to pay the filing fees and sheriff's fees, as well as the amount owed to you.

In addition to the filing fee, there will be a fee for serving papers on the defendants. If this is done by certified or registered mail, the fee is $3 to $6 per person. If they are served by a sheriff, the fee is currently $20. The fee must be paid twice to serve both a husband and wife, even if the sheriff makes only one trip to the house and gives both sets of papers to one person. If the sheriff cannot find the party, or if you expect the party to hide from the sheriff, you can hire a private process server which may cost a bit more than the sheriff.

If you are *indigent*, that is, if you do not have any money available to pay the court costs, they may be waived by the court. To request a waiver you should file an AFFIDAVIT OF INABILITY TO PAY COSTS from this book or the equivalent form available at your courthouse. (see form 20, p.126.) You must be honest in filling out this form or you may be held in contempt of court or prosecuted for perjury. Do not claim to be indigent if you are not legally so.

AMOUNT TO SUE FOR

When filing a suit you should always ask for the highest amount imaginable for the claim.

Example: If someone hit your car and you got estimates of $200, $300 and $450 to fix it, you might be happy if the person paid you $200. If they are offering to settle the case for that you should probably accept it. But if you have to sue them for it, sue for $450, plus any other amounts you can reasonably add to the bill, such as taxi fare home from the repair shop, lost time at work, lost use of the car, etc.

You might not get these amounts, but they will give you room for negotiation. If you sue for $450 and are willing to settle for $200, the defendant would be well advised to pay the $200.

Example: Suppose you paid $500 for an old oil painting and the seller failed to deliver it because he sold it to someone else for $1000. Rather than suing for your $500 back you should sue for the $1000 which is the value you lost due to the seller's breach.

OTHER REMEDIES YOU CAN ASK FOR

SPECIFIC PERFORMANCE

In some cases money is not an adequate remedy. For example, in the oil painting example in the last section, if the seller had not yet sold the painting, you could sue him for *specific performance* which means you ask the judge to force him to deliver the goods.

MUTUAL MISTAKE

If a deal was made under a *mutually mistaken* assumption or under duress (see the explanation for these in the next chapter) you could sue for *rescission* of the contract. Recission is the canceling of a contract and putting the parties back in their original pre-contract positions.

RESTITUTION

If an item was not paid for you could ask for *restitution*, meaning it would be returned to you. Getting an item back is often better than getting a money judgment that will never be paid.

REFORMATION

Where a written agreement does not express the true understanding of the parties, a court can *reform* the contract to express their intent.

Example: If you sign a receipt to sell a 1988 auto to your neighbor and accidentally write 1998, you probably won't have to deliver a 1998 car to him. If he sued for that you could ask the judge to *reform* the contract to reflect the correct date.

THE BEGINNING

To begin your case, you must file a *statement of claim*. First, you must decide what type of suit it is and choose the appropriate form. In many counties the clerks have ready-to-use forms and they will help you fill them out. However, if such forms are not available or if the forms do not fit the facts of your case, you can use the forms in this book. (see forms 1 through 18.)

The following is an explanation of the types of suits that are usually brought before a small claims court, and the necessary elements of each. Even if you can prove all of the elements, you should check all of the defenses in Chapter 4 to see if the defendant will be able to use any of them to bar your claim. Also, be sure to check the rules of evidence in Chapter 7 to see if you have the proper evidence to win your case.

REPLEVIN: RETURN OF PROPERTY

Replevin is an action to recover a piece of personal property that a person refuses to return to you. To win a replevin action you must prove a legal right to the possession of the property, such as ownership of it, and that the defendant wrongfully has possession of it.

There are three different replevin forms. The correct one to use depends upon the circumstances of your case. The generic form is form 1 in this book and is used for any type of replevin actions that cannot use the other two types of replevin forms (form 2 and form 3).

REPLEVIN: RETURN OF STOLEN PROPERTY FROM SECOND HAND DEALER

Replevin under Florida Statute, Section 538.08 is covered by form 2. This is a special action for return of certain stolen property that is in the hands of a "second hand dealer" such as a pawn shop, consignment shop, or garage sale operator. (For more specific information see Fla. Stat., Chapter (Ch.) 538. Section 538.03 lists what goods are included.) For this type of action the clerk must waive the filing fee and the sheriff must waive his service fee.

REPLEVIN: RETURN OF STOLEN METALS FROM RECYCLER

Replevin under Florida Statute, Section 538.24 is covered by form 3. This is a special action for return of stolen property from a "secondary metals recycler." (For more specific information see Fla. Stat., Secs. 538.18 through 538.26.) For this type of action the clerk must waive the filing fee and the sheriff must waive his service fee.

| ACCOUNT STATED | *Account stated* is an action to recover money owed on an account where the parties agreed to a balance but the customer never paid. (see form 4, p.108.) To win an account case, you must prove: |

1. the parties had previous dealings that were always paid or quickly questioned;

2. a statement for the claimed amount was rendered;

3. the defendant did not object to the statement which raised a presumption of assent; and,

4. the defendant never paid.

The advantage to this claim over a suit for payment for the goods themselves is that with this claim the other side cannot bring up the quality of the goods as a defense.

It may seem unfair, but by not objecting to an incorrect bill, a person agrees to pay it, and may be legally bound to pay it even if it is wrong. For customers, this means it is important to always question incorrect bills immediately; for businesses, it means it is important to send out regular statements.

NOTE: *All four elements must be present to win this action. If the defendant disproves one of the elements you will lose. If this type of claim does not fit your situation, you may want to file the next type of complaint, or to file a complaint using combined claim. (see form 7.)*

| OPEN ACCOUNT | This is an action to recover money owed on an open account, such as when a customer receives goods or services and is rendered a monthly bill. This is easier to collect than to sue for the value of the goods or services because if a person gets several regular bills and does not object to them, they can't contest the value of the services later. To win a suit on an open account you must prove: |

1. the defendant had a charge account;

2. a statement was rendered;

3. the amount of the balance; and,

4. it was never paid. (see form 5.)

If you are not sure you can prove all the elements for an open account claim, you might want to file a claim using three different alternate claims, in the expectation that at least one of them will be successful. (see form 7.)

GOODS OR SERVICES SOLD

This is an action to recover money owed for goods or services sold. To win a suit for goods or services sold, you must be able to identify the goods or services and prove:

1. the defendant purchased them;

2. a price was agreed to; and,

3. the goods or services were never paid for.

If no price was agreed to, then you must prove the reasonable value of the goods or services. (see form 6.)

GOODS OR SERVICES SOLD/ACCOUNT STATED/OPEN ACCOUNT

If you are not sure if you have the evidence to prove any one of the previous three claims, then you should consider filing a three-count claim. In this claim you alternately claim each of the three *grounds* for collection. If your evidence is insufficient for one, you still have a chance to prevail under another. Of course, you cannot collect triple the amount of the debt. (see form 7.)

IMPROPER SERVICES

This is an action to recover money that was paid for services that were not performed properly. To win a suit for improper services, unless it is obvious that the service was improper, you must provide an expert witness who can testify the services actually were improper. The expert must be someone trained in the field of those services who examined the matter in the suit. For example, if a new roof leaked the day after it was installed, it would probably be obvious that it was improperly done. But if you feel your car was not working properly after it was serviced, you would need another mechanic to testify that the repairs were done incorrectly. (see form 8.)

PROMISSORY
NOTE

This is an action to recover money owed on a promissory note which has not been paid on maturity. To win a suit on a note, you must prove:

1. the defendant executed the note;

2. it is past due;

3. demand for payment was made; and,

4. it was not paid. (see form 9.)

You should also make sure that documentary stamps have been paid on the note. These can be purchased from the court clerk. If you loaned someone money but did not have them sign a note, you can still sue them for the loan but you should use the miscellaneous claim form. (see form 18.)

UNPAID RENT

This is an action to recover rent from a tenant. To collect unpaid rent you must prove:

1. there was a written or oral agreement to pay a sum of rent; and

2. the defendant breached the agreement by failing to pay. (see form 10.)

This is not an *eviction* action. It is only for collection of money and is usually used to collect unpaid rent after the tenant has left. To evict a tenant you must file an eviction action in county court (not in the Small Claims Division).

DAMAGE TO
PREMISES

This is an action by a landlord to recover money for damage to rental premises and may include a claim for unpaid rent. (see form 11.) To collect for damage to premises, you must prove that the damages were done by the tenant or during the tenant's term of occupancy. This means you must have witnesses who saw the premises before and after the tenant took possession.

Photographs are very useful to a judge in such a case. Normal wear and tear is not considered damages, so if you have to repaint the property or clean the carpeting after a tenant has lived there several years, that would be normal expenses of being a landlord and not the tenant's liability. Like unpaid rent, this is not an eviction action.

SECURITY DEPOSIT

This is an action to recover a security deposit that was kept by a landlord. To win a return of a security deposit you must prove:

1. a deposit was paid and

2. either the landlord failed to make a claim on the deposit by certified mail within fifteen days of the day you vacated the premises, or (if the landlord did make a claim) that you properly objected to the claim. (Fla Stat., Sec. 83.49.)

NOTE: *If you left the premises before the end of the rental agreement, the landlord does not have to send the notice by certified mail. The landlord will have to pay your attorney fees if you successfully sue for return of a deposit, so you may as well hire an attorney if he or she will work on a contingent fee. (see form 12.)*

BAD CHECK

This is an action to collect on a check that was worthless because of insufficient funds or any other reason. After you have received a worthless check, you must first present it to a bank and have them mark on it the reason it was not paid. It is not enough to call the bank and ask if there is enough money to cover it. Then, you should send a **BAD CHECK NOTICE** by certified mail, return receipt requested, to the person who wrote the check. It does not matter if you know that he will refuse the letter; you must mail it anyway and keep the mailing receipt as well as the notice if it is returned to you by the post office. (see form 13B, p.119.) Certified letters may be sent by dropping them in the mail without having the receipt postmarked. However, this is not good proof of mailing unless the card is signed and returned to you, so be sure to have your receipt postmarked.

When a person gives you a bad check, you are entitled to charge them a service charge of $25 if the face amount does not exceed $50, $30 if the face amount exceeds $50 but does not exceed $300, or $40 if the face amount exceeds $300. If you must file a suit on a bad check you are entitled to receive triple the amount of the check with a minimum of $50 for small checks, in addition to the amount of the check, the service charge, court costs, attorney fees and bank fees. However you do not get all these extra amounts unless you send a special bad check notice by certified mail. Also, if the person pays the check, service charge, bank fees, court costs, attorney fees and other collection charges, he does not have to pay the triple damages.

The notice is included in this book. (see form 13B, p.119.) Thirty days after the person receives the notice you can file your suit. (see form 13A, p.118.) If the person refuses to sign for the notice you can file your suit once you receive the envelope back marked "refused." If you do not send the notice you can only sue for the amount of the check. (see form 13, p.117.)

BREACH OF
CONTRACT
This is an action to recover money damages for failure of a party to abide by the terms of an oral or written contract. To win a suit for breach of contract you must prove:

1. there was a written or oral agreement between the parties;

2. the defendant did not perform or performed improperly; and,

3. you performed or were ready, willing and able to perform your part of the agreement. (see form 14, p.120.)

AUTO
ACCIDENT
This is an action to recover money for damages sustained in an automobile accident. To win a claim for damages from an automobile accident, you must be able to prove:

1. the defendant caused some damage; and

2. it was done negligently (or intentionally).

To prove negligence you can use a guilty plea as evidence, but you cannot use a conviction of a traffic violation. (The reason people plead *nolo contendere* is that it is not a guilty plea which could be used against them). However, you can use the same witnesses as in the traffic case, and if you can prove the other party violated a traffic law, that would usually be proof of negligence. (see form 15, p.121.)

FOREIGN
JUDGMENT

This is an action to have an out-of-state judgment filed as a Florida judgment. To have the judgment filed in Florida, you must take a certified copy of it to the clerk of the circuit court and pay the filing fee. A notice is then sent to the debtor and he has thirty days in which to contest the filing. (see form 16, p.122.) If the judgment is from a foreign country, there is a new procedure that does not involve court action. Check with the court clerk for more information.

BREACH OF
EXPRESS
WARRANTY

This is a claim for damages when a product or service does not live up to an expressly worded warranty. To win such a case, a person must prove:

1.   there really was a warranty given (written or oral);

2.   the product or service breached the warranty; and,

3.   some damages resulted from the breach. (see form 17, p.123.)

MISCELLANEOUS
CLAIM

If your claim does not fit into any of the above claims, you can usually use a miscellaneous claim form. (see form 18, p.124.) One example of a miscellaneous claim would be a claim for money loaned if you do not have a note. Yes, you can collect money loaned without a note if you can convince the judge that a loan actually was made. Evidence you might use would be a cancelled check, the receipt from a money order, or a letter from the person asking for or thanking you for the loan.

Another type of claim that can be made on the miscellaneous claim form is one for implied warranty as discussed below.

BREACH OF
IMPLIED
WARRANTY

One good catch-all claim is for *implied warranty*. This is a claim used when a product or service does not fulfill its basic purpose. To make a claim for implied warranty you can use the miscellaneous claim form and recite the necessary elements. There are three types of implied warranties.

Warranty of Title. If you were sold an item that the seller did not own and that you had to return to the rightful owner (such as stolen property), you could sue the seller for breach of the implied warranty that he had title to the property he sold you. To do so you must prove:

1.   you paid for the item and

2.   you did not obtain title to it.

Warranty of Merchantability. When goods are sold by a dealer in such merchandise, unless they are sold "as is," there is an implied warranty that they are fit for the purpose for which they are made. If a washing machine does not wash, it is not merchantable. If bread is moldy, it is not merchantable. To win a claim for breach of the warranty of merchantability, you must prove that the goods were not merchantable when received.

If, for example, a car broke down two weeks after it was purchased, you could not collect for breach of such a warranty unless you could prove that at the time of the sale the car was in such a condition as to make it unmerchantable. If a part was ready to break, you would probably win. If it broke because you hit a bad bump in the road, you would probably lose.

Warranty of Fitness for a Particular Purpose. When a seller represents himself as being knowledgeable about a product and sells it to a person for a known particular purpose, there is an implied warranty of fitness for that purpose.

Example: If a body building gym sells a piece of pipe for use as a weight lifting bar and it bends, there would be a breach of a warranty even if it was a perfectly good pipe for other purposes.

To win a suit for an implied warranty, you need to prove that the seller was knowledgeable about the product and also about your reason for needing it.

QUANTUM MERUIT
One legal theory that could be used either under a breach of contract or miscellaneous claim is *quantum meruit*, which means the amount earned.

Example: If your neighbor asks you to fix his car and says he'll pay you what it's worth, and after buying $150 in parts and spending ten hours he gives you $50, you could sue him under quantum meruit for the $150 plus the fair value of your services.

NEGLIGENCE
A common problem that does not have its own form is *negligence*. This is where someone does some careless act that causes injury to your person or property. Automobile accidents are the most common types of

negligence and there is a special form for these as explained earlier in this chapter. However there are other types of negligence such as someone cutting down a tree and having it fall on your property causing damage, a child breaking a window with a baseball or a person draining their swimming pool and allowing the chlorinated water to flow into your yard killing your grass.

In order for a person to be liable for negligence four factors must be present.

1.   There must be a duty, such as a duty to be careful when cutting a tree limb or draining a pool.

2.   There must be a breach of that duty.

3.   There must be some damage. If your neighbor floods your yard and it causes no damage and does not inconvenience you in any way you are not entitled to collect damages because you have none.

4.   The person you are suing must have caused the damages.

Example: If a tree is perfectly healthy but a tornado pushes it into your neighbor's house you are not liable just for owning the tree. Since you did nothing to cause the damage you would not be legally liable.

MALPRACTICE
Malpractice is the type of claim you would make against a doctor, lawyer, accountant, or other professional whose error has cost you money or other losses. Small claims court may be the only option for people who have been a victim of malpractice for relatively small matters since the time involved in such a claim is not worth the time for most attorneys. However, just because you have had a bad result in a matter you brought to a professional does not mean there was malpractice.

Example 1:Suppose you went to a doctor for minor surgery and were left with an ugly scar you were not expecting. If the scar was caused by some error made by the doctor then he or she might be liable. But if the scar resulted from your body's failure to heal properly or from your failure to change your bandages as instructed, then the doctor would not be liable.

Example 2: Suppose you hire a lawyer to sue the doctor and lose. The lawyer is not necessarily liable if the judge or jury did not believe your side of the story. Only if he or she made some professional error would there be liability.

Whether or not there has been liability is a difficult question and requires the opinion of experts in the field. If you bring a suit for malpractice you will most likely need to hire at least one *expert witness.* (see Chapter 7.)

To find out if you have a good case you should get the opinion of an attorney who specializes in malpractice. Most attorneys in this area will give an initial consultation at no charge. If they think you have a good case they might offer to handle it for you, or if the case is too small to merit their full time they might might agree to consult on the case.

If the attorney says that you do not have a good case, consider that your chances of recovery are probably slim and it may not be worth your time to file a suit.

LEMON LAW   Florida has a *lemon law* covering new automobiles that have manufacturing defects that cannot be fixed. Since no new cars cost less than $5000 today, this law would probably not be useful in small claims court. If a used car is a lemon, you may be able to sue for misrepresentation or for breach of an implied warranty. If a dealer fails to repair a vehicle properly, you can sue for services performed improperly.

ATTACHMENTS TO THE CLAIM

If you are basing your claim on a written document such as a lease, contract, or written warranty, you must attach a copy of it to your claim. (Keep the original for evidence at the hearing.) If you have other documents, such as letters or estimates, do not attach them to the complaint, but plan to bring them to court as evidence.

POSSIBLE DEFENSES

Before you file a case you should consider whether the defendant has any valid defenses or a counterclaim against you. You should review Chapter 4 of this book to see if your claim would be barred by some legal rule. Consider any claims a defendant might be able to make against you. Occasionally, a person filing a small claim ends up losing a lot more than he was suing for.

JURY TRIAL

If you wish to have your case heard by a jury, you need to request a jury trial at the time you file your claim. However, a jury trial is not recommended because it is expensive, time consuming and usually does not give you any advantage over a trial before a judge. The judge will be experienced with similar cases and will usually be just as impartial as any jury.

SERVING THE PAPERS

Once the statement of claim is filed it must be *served* on each defendant. You will need to have one extra copy for each person you are suing, including one copy of each attachment. Service can be done by registered or certified mail or by having a deputy sheriff hand deliver the papers. The cost of having the papers delivered by a deputy is higher than by mail, but a person can refuse to accept the papers by mail, especially if he or she expects that you will be suing him or her. If they are refused, you will then have to request that an "alias" (duplicate) summons be issued and hire the sheriff or a process server to serve it.

You should give the sheriff the best address and directions available. If the sheriff cannot find the defendant, you will have to pay another fee for the sheriff to try again, after you find a new address. You should supply home and work addresses for the person, along with a brief description, if you think the person will lie about who he is.

If the sheriff cannot find the defendant, you will have to file a REQUEST FOR ALIAS OR PLURIES SERVICE and provide a new address. (see form 21, p.127.) The clerk will then send a new summons to the sheriff to be served.

If the defendant is hard to locate, you might want to hire a private process server. Sometimes the cost is the same as the sheriff, sometimes more. You should look in the Yellow Pages under "Process Servers" or "Detective Agencies." A motion and order must be presented to the judge to allow a process server to serve papers. Some process servers have their own forms, but a sample is included in this book. (see form 19, p.125.)

DEFENDING YOURSELF 4

If you are sued in small claims court, you should read all of the documents carefully to find out where to appear in court and what you are being sued for.

If you know the claim is true, you should contact the other party and try to settle the matter. You should not waste the court's time and incur additional expenses if you know you owe the money you are being sued for. If you do not have the money, you could offer to sign a promissory note to make regular payments or you could sign a stipulation in the court case to make payments.

IGNORING A SUMMONS

You should *never* ignore a summons that comes to you from a court. There have been cases where wealthy individuals have ignored suits that they thought were silly and then lost great amounts of property when the court seized their buildings to pay off judgments as small as $100. If you cannot make the hearing, you can ask for a continuance or hire a lawyer to represent you. (see form 30, p.136.)

YOUR DEFENSES

Before you decide to settle the case you should review your defenses in the matter and see if the claim is legally enforceable. There are many possible defenses to a claim which you (and the plaintiff) may not know about.

Read all of the following possible defenses and see if any of them apply to your case. If you think any might, be sure to mention them to the judge if your case does go to court. Some of the defenses may just delay the case, and if you are in a hurry to get it over with you might not want to use them, even if they do apply. But many of them are defenses that could win the case for you.

IMPROPER SERVICE OF PROCESS

If the statement of claim is not served on you properly then the court does not have jurisdiction and the judgment is void. However, if you appear in court and do not object to the service then you waive the right to contest it.

Improper service may be by mailing or delivering the STATEMENT OF CLAIM to the wrong address, or not naming you properly. If service is improper you have two choices. You can ignore it or you can appear only for the purpose of contesting the service. If you ignore it, you may have more aggravation later in having a judgment set aside or in trying to stop seizure of your property. If you appear to contest the service, you may be able to have the service set aside so that the plaintiff has to start over and hire the sheriff to find you. But then, you may just aggravate the judge who will eventually hear your case. In deciding what to do, you should consult a book on civil procedure such as *Trawick's Florida Practice and Procedure*, by Henry Trawick.

VENUE

Are you being sued in the right court? See Chapter 3, "Where to File Your Suit", to find out if you are being sued in the right court. If not, you might be able to have the case moved (or you might prefer not to). This may just delay the case, but perhaps the plaintiff will drop the case if he or she has to travel to another county. You must bring up the venue issue at your first appearance or it may be waived.

DENIAL

First read the statement of claim and all exhibits carefully to see if everything is true. Look at your records and compare the dates and other details. Perhaps the claim is untrue. If an important aspect of the claim is untrue, you may win the case.

UNSUPPORTED CLAIMS

The Florida legislature recently expanded Florida Statute, Section 57.105 to increase the penalties for filing a lawsuit without a good basis. If a judge finds a claim was filed without basis, he or she can award you damages and attorney fees if you hire an attorney to defend you.

CORPORATE REGISTRATION

If the plaintiff is a corporation, it must be current in its registration to maintain a suit. You can call the Secretary of State in Tallahassee 850-488-9000 to check on a corporation's status. If it is not current, you can order a certificate of proof of non-active status for about $5 from the following address:

Secretary of State
Corporate Records Bureau
P. O. Box 6327
Tallahassee, FL 32301

This information is also available on the internet at:

http://ccfcorp.dos.state.fl.us/index/html

This may only delay the suit, but if the corporation is a few years behind in filing, it may be too much trouble and expense to file and then start up the suit again. The fees are hundreds of dollars to reinstate a corporation.

NONRESIDENT BOND

If the plaintiff is not a resident of Florida, the Florida Statute says that he must post a $100.00 bond to cover possible costs. (Fla. Stat., Sec. 57.011.) You can mention this to the judge and this may buy you some time, or the plaintiff might just give up.

FICTITIOUS NAMES

If the plaintiff is using a fictitious name that is not registered, then he may not bring a suit. This will usually just delay the case a couple of months while the plaintiff is publishing the ad and filing the registration. But again, the plaintiff may feel it is too much trouble and not go through with the case. In the past, names were registered in each county. Later, they may have been registered with either the county or the Secretary of State. However, now they must be registered with the Secretary of State. You can check with the Official Records office in your county courthouse and the Secretary of State's office (address and phone number are located on the previous page) to see if a name is registered.

RES JUDICATA

This is an old legal rule meaning that the case has already been decided. There can only be one case on each single controversy. If a court already considered a matter, a new court cannot reopen it.

Example: If you sued a tenant for an eviction under a lease, he can't bring a new case later claiming you violated the lease. He should have brought up the matter as a counterclaim in the original suit.

LACK OF
CONSIDERATION

Promises to make gifts are not enforceable. Therefore, if you signed a promise to pay someone and never received anything in return, the promise would be unenforceable. This can be used in many kinds of cases.

Example 1: If you promised to give your neighbors your old car when you got a new one, they could not win a suit for the car if you changed your mind, since they didn't do anything for the car. However, if you told them you would give them your old car if they mowed your lawn every week, and they did mow your lawn, then they could sue you and win.

Example 2: If you agreed to pay $1000 for a diamond ring and signed a promissory note to the seller, then discovered the stone to be glass, you could probably avoid paying the note because you got nothing for it. (You could probably also use the fraud or the mutual mistake defenses). However, if you borrowed the money from a third party such as a bank, you could probably not avoid repaying the bank for the loan because the bank is not responsible for the condition of the item you bought.

Also, if you bought something and signed a promissory note and then the dealer sold the note to a bank or other lender, you could probably not avoid paying the note, since the bank would be considered an innocent buyer of the note and the law encourages the easy sale of "commercial paper." Many businesses that sell questionable products quickly sell the loan papers so that the buyers cannot stop payment. Sometimes the bank or other lender can lose the case if they are part of a conspiracy with the business, but this type of case would be difficult to prove.

STATUTE OF FRAUDS

Certain agreements are not enforceable if they are not in writing. Even if the facts are true and money is owed, the *Statute of Frauds* provide that these agreements just will not be enforced by the court if they are not written and signed. The writing need not be a formal contract. Cancelled checks and short memoranda signed by one party have, in some cases, been held to be sufficient. The following are the instances when the agreement must be in writing. For further research, the statute citations are included with each.

- Sales of any interest in real estate (Fla. Stat., Sec. 689.01 and Sec. 725.01);

- Leases of real estate of over one year (Fla. Stat., Sec. 725.01);

- Guarantees of debts of another person (Fla. Stat., Sec. 725.01);

- Guarantee by administrator of debts of an estate (Fla. Stat., Sec. 725.01);

- Subscriptions to newspapers and periodicals (Fla. Stat., Sec. 725.03);

- Sales of goods over $500 (Fla. Stat., Sec. 672.201) as defined in Florida Statutes, Section 672.105;

- Sales of certain personal property such as royalty rights or contract rights over $5,000 (Fla. Stat., Sec. 671.206);

- Transfers of security interests (Fla. Stat., Sec. 679.2031);

- Agreements which take longer than one year to complete (Fla. Stat., Sec. 725.01);

- Commercial leases (Fla. Stat., Sec. 680.201); or,

- Guarantees by physicians, osteopaths, chiropractors or dentists for certain results (Fla. Stat., Sec. 725.01).

This means that if you agree to buy a car for $6000, you cannot be forced to go through with the deal unless the agreement is in writing. However, if you signed a $100 check and wrote on it "Deposit on Chevy," or if you started driving the car, the agreement might be taken out of the Statute of Frauds and be enforceable.

MINORS An agreement entered into by a minor is generally not enforceable in court. The exceptions to this are if the minor continues to fulfill the agreement after reaching majority or if the agreement was for a *necessity*. Thus, if a minor signed an agreement to buy a car, it would probably not be enforceable, but if he signed a check to pay for food it probably would be.

PAYMENT Obviously, if you have already paid the money claimed to be owed, this would be a defense to the claim. Perhaps the money was credited to a wrong account or not credited at all. To prevail with this defense you should have some evidence that you have made payment, such as a cancelled check or a receipt.

ACCORD & SATISFACTION If a debt is in dispute and the parties agree to a settlement, such as acceptance of 50% of the debt, this should finally settle the matter. If one party later claims the whole amount in a suit, the settlement agreement would be a defense. This agreement of *accord and satisfaction* should be in writing, but even if it is not, it may be enforceable.

PAYMENT AFTER SUIT IS FILED Once a suit is filed, the loser will usually have to pay the court costs in addition to the money owed. This usually consists of the filing fee and the sheriff's fee. If the amount owed is in dispute, the defendant can pay what he thinks he owes into the registry of the court and if the judgment is not for a greater amount, he will not have to pay the court costs.

STATUTE OF
LIMITATIONS

The laws of every state give time limits on how long claims can be brought. After a certain time, claims will not be allowed by the court, no matter how valid they are. Thus, if a person waits too long to file a suit, his or her claim may not be enforceable. The time limit for most kinds of claims is four years. Some of the exceptions are as follows.

- Actions to collect on recorded Florida judgments: twenty years (Fla. Stat., Sec. 95.11(1));

- Action to collect on unrecorded judgments: five years (Fla. Stat., Sec. 95.11(2)(a));

- Actions based on a written agreement: five years (Fla. Stat., Sec. 95.11(2)(b));

- Mortgage foreclosures: five years (Fla. Stat., Sec. 95.11(2)(c));

- Malpractice by professionals: two years (Fla. Stat., Sec. 95.11(4)(a));

- Medical malpractice: two years (Fla. Stat., Sec. 95.11(4)(b));

- Action for wages: two years (Fla. Stat., Sec. 95.11(4)(c));

- Actions for wrongful death: two years (Fla. Stat., Sec. 95.11(4)(d));

- Violations of securities laws: two years (Fla. Stat., Sec. 95.11(4)(e));

- Actions for specific performance: one year (Fla. Stat., Sec. 95.11(5)(a));

- Actions to enforce equitable liens for improvement of real property: one year (Fla. Stat., Sec. 95.11(5)(b));

- Actions on bulk transfers under the Uniform Commercial Code: one year (Fla. Stat., Sec. 95.11(5)(c));

- Actions against guaranty associations and their insured: one year (Fla. Stat., Sec. 95.11(5)(d)); or,

- Actions against payment bonds under the construction lien law: one year (Fla. Stat., Sec. 95.11(5)(e)).

In some cases, it is tricky to figure out when the time period starts. For professional malpractice, the two years usually starts running from when the cause of action is discovered or should have been discovered. So, if a person should have known his doctor made an error, but did not actually discover it until three years later, the claim would be barred.

If you think you have a good statute of limitations defense, you should check the latest Florida Statutes and bring a photocopy of the applicable section to court. Most sections on limitations are in Chapter 95 of the Florida Statutes, but you want to also check the index to the statutes under *Limitations of Actions* to see if there are any special rules for your type of case.

FRAUD OR MISREPRESENTATION
If you were defrauded in a transaction, or if important facts were misrepresented to you, you may have a valid defense. For example, if you bought a car and later found out the odometer was set back, you can use that as a defense if you are sued for the price of the car. Usually though, such claims should be used for a counterclaim. (see Chapter 6.)

MISTAKE OR ERROR
If both parties were mistaken about an agreement they entered into, it can usually be voided.

Example: If both parties believed a gem to be a diamond, but it turned out to be a fake, then a sale of it could be rescinded. If only the seller knew it was a fake, this defense would not work, but the fraud defense might.

BREACH OF CONTRACT
If the plaintiff did not fulfill his side of an agreement, he may not be able to sue you to collect on it. Thus, if improper goods or services were provided, the seller should not be able to collect.

Example: If you hired someone to paint your house and they did a sloppy job, or if you contracted for a catering service for a wedding and they showed up four hours late, they would have breached the contract.

In the painting example, you can also argue that they breached an implied warranty to do the job in a workmanlike manner (see the next section). Explain to the judge any ways that the plaintiff failed to fulfill his side of the agreement.

IMPLIED WARRANTIES

Even if a provider of goods and services does not provide a written warranty, the law implies three types of warranties in most business transactions. These are:

1. that the seller of goods actually owns them and can legally sell them;

2. that the the goods or services are merchantable, that is that they perform the function they are supposed to; and,

3. if the seller is knowledgeable about them and sells them for a particular purpose that they will fulfill that purpose.

USURY

If you were loaned money at an annual interest rate of over 18% per year, there may have been a violation of the *usury* laws. If so, you would only be required to pay back the principle without interest. In extreme cases, such as if the interest amounted to 45% per year or more, the lender may have to pay you a penalty. Florida's usury laws are found in Chapter 687 of the Florida Statutes.

ARBITRATION

To avoid litigation, many parties are putting *arbitration* clauses in their contracts. These clauses provide that the parties agree that in the event of a dispute under the contract they agree not to file suit but to go to an arbitrator. There are different versions of these clauses. Some of them require that arbitration be tried before suit is filed. Others say that the arbitrators decision will be final. If the contract being sued on has such a clause, the judge may be required to dismiss the case if the clause has not been followed. Of course if a party is suing about a matter which is not covered under the contract, then the clause would not apply.

DURESS

If an agreement is made under *duress*, then it may not be enforceable.

Example: If someone confronts you with a gun and says "sign your house over to me or I will shoot you," you could stop payment on the check since your agreement would have been given under duress.

Duress has to be serious, however. If a mechanic says he will not return your car unless you pay for it and you pay because you need the car even though you feel the work was done wrong, this might not be considered to be duress because you have other options. For example, you could have sued to get your car back. But small claims court judges are flexible and it might work in a car case.

ILLEGALITY   Agreements that are illegal cannot be enforced in court. If you write a check to pay for illegal drugs, or prostitution, or illegal gambling, the court will not help the person you paid collect the check.

LICENSE   In certain situations people can give up their right to sue by granting a written or an implied license to the other person. For example, if two people agree to have a boxing match, one of them cannot later sue the other for battery if he is hurt. By agreeing to participate in a fight he impliedly gave the other person a license to hit him. If the fight were under the auspices of a club or organization, the parties were probably required to sign an agreement which contained a license as well as a waiver of the right to sue.

WAIVER   As discussed in the previous paragraph, in some cases people waive their right to sue. Restaurants, bars, social clubs, and other groups which hold any types of contests usually require all participants to sign *waivers* of their right to sue. The participants are usually too excited about entering the contest to read what they are signing, but if they try to go to court they learn that they have waived their right to sue.

RELEASE   Similar to a waiver is a *release*.

Example: Suppose a landlord and a tenant get into a lawsuit with both making claims against the other. They do not want to take a chance in court so they agree to settle. They both sign releases of the other and dismiss the case. If six months later the tenant finds a cash receipt proving that he paid more rent than he realized, he probably would not be able to sue because he already signed a release.

Such releases typically include language that they release all claims "from the beginning of the world until this date…," so even if the tenant later realized he had some other problem, such as lead poison from the pipes on the property, he would most likely be out of luck.

DOCUMENTARY TAX STAMPS

If the *documentary stamp tax* (a tax on legal instruments such as deeds and promissory notes) has not been paid on a promissory note, the court will not enforce it. By bringing this up at a trial, you should win. However, the judge may allow the plaintiff to dismiss his suit and to refile it after buying documentary stamps. If you pay the debt in the meantime, you might be able to avoid paying court costs.

SALES OF GOODS

Sales of goods are governed by a set of laws called the Uniform Commercial Code (Fla. Stat., Ch. 672). If you are being sued over a transaction involving a sale of goods, there might be some rule which covers your case. For example, if you sold defective goods and the buyer did not give you proper notice that they were defective, then he may not be able to win a suit against you.

BANKRUPTCY

If a person files *liquidation bankruptcy*, the debts listed can be wiped out and completely discharged forever. If a person files a bankruptcy petition while a case is pending, all actions against the person and his property must stop. If you are the plaintiff, and a defendant tells you that he has filed bankruptcy, you should call the local federal bankruptcy court to confirm that it has been filed. If you take any action after you have been informed of a bankruptcy, then you may be held in contempt of federal court.

In a *reorganization bankruptcy*, the debts will not be wiped out but the court will approve a schedule for payment of them. Still, a creditor may not take any actions against the debtor while he or she is in bankruptcy.

Settling the Case

Whether or not you have any defenses to the case, it is usually better to negotiate a settlement than to take a chance with a judge's decision. No matter how sure you are of your case, you can easily lose if your witness does not show up or if the other side is more believable, or if any number of things go wrong.

It is often better to take only a partial victory than to risk complete defeat. If the plaintiff understands that he may never be able to collect his judgment, he might accept 50¢ or even 25¢ on the dollar for a cash settlement.

Even if you know you owe the full amount, you should try to avoid a judgment being issued against you. This will be damaging to your credit rating. The best arrangement for both sides is to enter into a STIPULATION TO STAY ENTRY OF JUDGMENT. This is an agreement by which the parties agree that if the defendant makes payments according to a certain schedule, no judgment will be entered. It is important for the defendant to keep payment by the schedule or else the judgment will be quickly filed. If the payments are made, no judgment will ever be filed. (see form 28, p.134.)

Some counties have dispute settlement programs where parties can talk to a mediator and avoid the trouble of court. But such mediation is not binding, and a person who does not get his way may go to court anyway.

COUNTERSUING 5

The best defense is a good offense, so the best way to defend yourself is to find a reason to sue the plaintiff. If there is only a suit pending against you, the plaintiff will be eager to try the case because he or she can either win or not win. But if you file a suit, he or she may lose. When both parties have claims against each other, the cases are often dropped or settled quickly because neither party wants to take a chance of losing.

COMPULSORY CLAIMS

If you have claims based upon the transaction that the plaintiff is suing over, then you must bring up these claims in the same case. If you do not, you will never be able to bring them up again in another suit.

Example: If a builder sues you for not paying a remodeling bill, you should sue him for any claims you have against him for defective work. If you just ignore his suit, or if you fail to bring up your claims, he may win and you will never be able to go after him for the defective work.

HOW TO COUNTERSUE

After you are served with a statement of claim and have reviewed all of the facts, you should check with the court clerk about filing a counterclaim. You may be able to file it immediately. But, in some counties, you may be given ten days by the judge at the pretrial hearing in which to file your counterclaim.

A counterclaim is just like an original STATEMENT OF CLAIM. (see form 23, p.129.) You should review Chapter 3 of this book regarding the preparation of a claim.

You should also review all the defenses in Chapter 4 to see if the plaintiff has a defense to your countersuit. But even if he or she does have a defense, make your claim anyway. They might not realize they have a defense and if they do not raise it they lose it.

EXCEEDING THE LIMIT

If you have a claim which is over $5000, it cannot be heard in small claims court. If your claim is between $5000 and $15,000, the case can remain in county court; but if it is over $15,000, it must be transferred to circuit court. You will usually need a lawyer if your claim is over $5000 because there are much stricter rules of procedure which must be followed.

If your claim is for over $5000, but you wouldn't mind limiting your judgment to $5000, you can continue the action in small claims court.

CROSSCLAIM AND THIRD PARTY CLAIM

If you are being sued in a matter and there is someone else involved who has some or all of the responsibility, then you should sue them.

If that person is already a defendant in the suit, you will need to file a crossclaim. (see form 24, p.130.) If that person is not a party to the suit, then you will have to bring them in as a third party defendant. (see form 22, p.128.)

Example: Suppose you were involved in an automobile accident where Car A hit you and pushed you into Car B. If you and the driver of Car A were sued by the driver of Car B, you should file a crossclaim against the driver of Car A. You would make a claim for damage to your car and for damage caused by your car hitting Car B.

If you alone were sued by the driver of Car B, then you would file a third party claim against the driver of Car A as a third party defendant.

In filing a crossclaim or third party claim, you take the position of a plaintiff. You should immediately contact the county clerk to find out the procedure in your county.

If you are filing a third party claim, you will have to have your statement of claim served upon the third party defendant just as if you were filing a new suit. This can be done by mail or by the sheriff. You should read the section in Chapter 3 on serving the papers for more details.

NOTE: *Be sure any claims you make are supported by the facts. Otherwise, you could be required to pay the other side's damages and attorney fees under Florida Statutes, Section 57.105.*

Your Pretrial Conference and Trial 6

The two appearances in court in a small claims court case are the pretrial conference and the trial. If you settle your case prior to either of these, you should contact the court to cancel them.

The Pretrial Conference

Prior to holding the trial, the small claims court judge, or someone appointed by the judge, holds a *pretrial conference*. The purpose of this is to dispense with cases in which the parties will not show up, to find out what the issues are and to prepare the parties for trial.

Sometimes at the pretrial conference the defendant will admit owing the debt but will say he just does not have any money. In such a case, a trial can be avoided if the defendant will sign a stipulation to pay the debt.

At the pretrial conference you can also find out if your opponent will have an attorney. If so, you should also consider having one. In some areas of Florida you can get a preliminary conference with an attorney for about $20 through the local Bar referral service. In areas without a local referral service you can call the Florida Bar statewide referral service. The number is 800-342-8011.

Recent changes in the Florida Small Claims Rules allow a party, witness, or attorney to be present over the telephone. If you will be out of town, or if your witness has to work, you may be able to have testimony taken over the phone. You might also consider having your attorney attend by telephone to avoid the cost of travel to the courthouse. This would probably cut the bill in half.

If you are considering any of these options, you should bring them up with the judge at the pretrial conference. Since these rules are new, the judge may be unfamiliar with them or may be uncomfortable using the telephone. The judge does not have to allow a person to appear by telephone, so don't press the matter.

To better understand the entire procedure and your rights, you may want to review the small claims court rules that are included in Appendix B.

SETTLING BEFORE TRIAL

Most lawyers will agree it is much better to settle a case and get most of what you want than to hold out for everything and have a trial. Even the most iron-clad cases have been lost at trial. There are many reasons for this. The judge may not believe you, your witness may get the facts mixed up, the judge may feel sorry for the other side, or there may be a little known legal rule precluding your recovery.

If you can come out ahead by settling for part of what you want, you should consider that option. If a tenant offers you $100 in back rent, but you feel he owes $400, you might be better off with $100 in cash than with a $400 judgment you may never collect. Weigh the chances of winning and the chances of actually collecting (and the time involved) with the amount the defendant is willing to settle for and decide if it's worth it.

If the problem is that the defendant has no money, you should consider a partial payment with a stipulation that the rest will be paid later as described on page 46. With this procedure you will get a judgment automatically if the defendant doesn't make the agreed payment.

DISMISSING THE CASE

If you have settled all issues in the case with the other party, you should dismiss the case. This is done using a NOTICE OF VOLUNTARY DISMISSAL. (see form 40, p.148.) If the other party has merely agreed to pay you but not actually paid, do not dismiss the case until full payment has been received.

JURY TRIAL

Jury trials are allowed in small claims court, but they are rarely used. Two reasons for this are that they are expensive and that juries are more unpredictable than judges. One judge can usually do as well as several jurors.

COURT REPORTERS

A *court reporter* is a person who attends a trial and records every word said. This is done so that if there is an appeal, the appeals court can review what was done at the trial. Having a court reporter attend the trial and transcribe the hearing is very expensive and most likely not worth it in a small claims case. However, if the amount involved is high and you want to guaranty your right to appeal if you lose, then you should ask at the pretrial conference about hiring a court reporter. In some counties you hire one yourself but in others it is done through the court. Be sure to read Chapter 9 about appeals before asking about a court reporter.

TRIAL

If you have not settled the case and if the defendant has not *defaulted* (failed to show up), then a trial will be held. The purpose of the trial is for the judge or jury to hear both sides of the case and decide who should win and what money, if any, is owed.

The trial is your only chance to present your case to the court. You cannot tell the judge that you are not ready or you forgot some of the evidence unless you have some sort of real emergency. If there is an emergency and you must leave town or your witness is unavailable, then you should immediately contact the judge or the court clerk. If you explain the situation to the judge's secretary or the clerk, it may be possible to delay the trial. Possibly you may be asked to file a MOTION FOR CONTINUANCE, and to set a hearing at which the motion will be considered. (see form 30, p.136.)

Different judges require differing degrees of formality in trial procedure. Some may follow a formal procedure while others may just informally ask each party for his or her side of the case. If the court follows formal procedure the trial will progress as follows:

1. opening remarks by the judge;

2. plaintiff's opening statement;

3. defendant's opening statement;

4. plaintiff's evidence;

5. defendant's evidence;

6. plaintiff's rebuttal and closing argument;

7. defendant's closing argument;

8. plaintiff's rebuttal to closing argument; and,

9. judge's decision.

Sometimes the judge does not make a decision in court, but waits a few days and mails out an opinion. There are reasons for this. Sometimes the judge wants to carefully examine or review the evidence or the case law. Other times the judge wants to give the parties time to calm down or wants to avoid a scene in the courtroom if he or she expects that.

"THE RULE"

There is a rule of court procedure that is so old that it is just called "the rule." It is the *rule of sequestration*. This is the rule that the witnesses may not be in the courtroom except when they are testifying and that they may not talk with each other. This is done so that each gives his own recollection of the events without influence from other witnesses. If you think it may help your case to have the witnesses testify separately (such as if you know they are making up a story), you may ask the judge to *invoke the rule*.

PREPARATION FOR TRIAL

You should prepare your case so you can present it quickly and in an orderly manner. The statement of claim forms include all the elements which you must prove to win your case. Read each statement on your STATEMENT OF CLAIM and be sure you have some proof for it.

Be sure you know in which courtroom your trial will be held. It may not be in the same room as the pretrial conference. In counties which have more than one courthouse be sure you know which courthouse to go to (even lawyers have been known to show up at the wrong courtroom).

You should be sure your witnesses will be available (see the next chapter) and be sure you know what their testimony will be. If they do not have a good memory of the facts, you may not want them to come to the trial. Be sure that your witnesses know where the courtroom is located. You may want to drive them to court so you are sure they will be there.

In many cases you will be required to provide to the other side a witness and evidence list ten days before trial. If you forget to do this, the court may refuse to hear your witnesses or to look at your evidence. The purpose of the list is to let each side know what he or she is up against. When you receive a list from the other side, review it and see if there are any surprises. Be sure you have enough evidence and witnesses to counter theirs. Lawyers usually wait until the last minute to hand over their list so that the other side cannot come up with last minute rebuttal witnesses.

PRESENTING YOUR CASE

While the rules of law are the basis for all court decisions, there are certain other factors which must be considered.

APPEARANCE

Appearance is important. An unshaven biker in court against an eighty-year-old widow in a wheelchair might have a hard time proving he is an innocent victim. Many judges consider shorts or tattered jeans disrespectful of the court system and might be prejudiced against a party because of such attire. On the other hand, if someone dresses too well and wears too much heavy gold jewelry, there might also be prejudice against that person.

ATTITUDE

One of the most important parts of the case other than the facts themselves is your attitude in court. If you sound sincere and are respectful to the judge, he or she will have more sympathy for your case than if you are rude and make it clear that you will not pay even if you lose.

PREPARATION

While you should be prepared for court, you should not bring prepared statements to be read. Make a list of the important points which you plan to cover and refer to your list to be sure that you do not miss any of them.

SPEAKING TO THE JUDGE

Pay attention to the judge's questions and answer them directly. If the judge does not seem to understand, ask him or her if you should explain. Do not ramble on about meaningless points. Do not say that everyone knows the defendant is a crook. Just explain the facts of your case. Listen carefully to what the judge is asking. It is often an important legal question that will decide the outcome of your case. If you do not understand the question, ask him or her to explain it.

Do not interrupt the other party and do not moan if they are lying. Be polite and wait for your turn to explain or to cross-examine them. While the other side is testifying you should take notes. If the other side lies about something or says something that needs to be explained, write it down. When the other side is done testifying, you will have a chance to *cross-examine*. At this point you can bring up statement inconsistencies.

CROSS-
EXAMINATION

The cross-examination is not the time to tell your side of the case. You must ask the other party questions. You should ask them questions that show flaws in their argument.

Example 1: Suppose you own a pool service and they claim you could never clean their pool right. You might ask them if they continuously used your services for five years. If they recommended you to other neighbors, then ask them about that.

Example 2: Suppose someone owes you money they say they never borrowed the money from you. Ask them why they were sending you checks every month.

RESPECT THE
OTHER PARTY

Only ask questions that will make them look bad. If they say you never made any repairs in the apartment, do not ask them what items you did not fix—they will make a long list and you will only look worse. Ask them, "Didn't I fix the faucet in April?," and "Didn't I fix the roof in June?"

LYING

Whatever you do, do not lie under oath. It is a criminal offense. If the other side lies, explain it to the judge when it is your turn to testify. If you explain your side truthfully, it will probably be more believable anyway.

WITNESSES

Use your witnesses to verify your side of the facts. Ask the witnesses questions that will lead to answers verifying your side of the facts. Tell the witness ahead of time to be brief and to only answer the questions asked of him. Tell him not to go into a long story unless asked to. If you have five witnesses to the same facts, ask the judge if he wants to hear all of them. If the defendant has no witnesses and you have five, the judge may only want to hear one or two, or may only have a single question for the other witnesses.

Sometimes a judge will tell you the other witnesses will not be necessary. Other times the judge will be noncommittal and say it is up to you. In the latter situation, your best bet would be to bring all of the witnesses in, but just ask each witness one or two key questions. If you waste a lot of time or make the judge miss lunch, he or she won't feel very kindly toward your view of the facts.

THE COURT'S RULING

After both sides have presented their cases the judge may immediately make a ruling and grant a judgment or he or she may say that the case will be *taken under advisement* which means he or she wants to think about it and mail a ruling to both sides.

One reason this may be done is that the judge may want to study the evidence closer or may want to look up the law on the matter. Another reason is that the parties may be showing a lot of emotion and the judge is afraid of an outburst.

Sometimes cases are taken under advisement for months. Judges get busy with other cases or are already backlogged. If you have not received a judgment a month or two after your trial, you might call the judge's office to see if the judgment was lost in the mail. However, do not act upset, or irritated with them because the if the judgment was not yet written you might hurt your case.

THE JUDGMENT

In most counties the judge will prepare a FINAL JUDGMENT. If the judge requires you to supply one, you can use form 46, p.155.

OPTIONAL ENFORCEMENT PARAGRAPH

The small claims court rules allow the judge to include an "optional enforcement paragraph" in a judgment. This paragraph orders the defendant to complete a lengthly questionnaire about his or her assets and is very helpful in collecting your judgment. The paragraph will not be included unless you ask for it so be sure to do so.

HEARING IN AID OF EXECUTION

Under Small Claims Rule 7.221 a judgment debtor may be ordered to appear at a Hearing in Aid of Execution. This is where you can ask him what assets he owns and get the numbers of his bank accounts and the location of his other assets so that you can have the sheriff seize them if he doesn't pay. He must bring to the hearing a Fact Information Sheet which lists all of his assets and it must be sworn to and notarized. Lying on this form is a crime.

If you did not get the Fact Information Sheet through the optional enforcement paragraph included in your judgment, you should file an EX PARTE MOTION FOR HEARING IN AID OF EXECUTION. (see form 38, p.145.)

STIPULATION TO STAY ENTRY OF JUDGMENT

If the judge makes a decision at the end of the trial, he or she may ask if the loser wants to pay before the judgment is entered, or if the parties want to stipulate to stay the entry of the judgment.

Under the first alternative, the judge wants to give the loser a chance to pay the money before a judgment is filed on his name. Under the second, the loser is given a chance to pay a little each week to avoid a judgment. For the defendant either of these is better than a judgment because a judgment looks bad on a person's credit report.

Often a plaintiff will want a lump settlement, not a little each month. But if the defendant does not have the money, it is often better to take small payments than a judgment that will never be collected.

To agree on a stipulation use the STIPULATION TO STAY ENTRY OF JUDGMENT. (see form 28, p.134.) If the defendant fails to make payments under the stipulation, use the AFFIDAVIT *(Balance Due on Stipulation)*. (see form 29, p.135.)

RULES OF EVIDENCE

In order to convince the judge that you should win your case, you must have adequate evidence that your claims are true. Although the small claims court is a simplified procedure, the standard rules of evidence still apply. Even if you are absolutely right, you will lose your case unless you have legal evidence.

HEARSAY RULE

The most basic rule of evidence is the *hearsay rule*. This is the rule that the court cannot accept any evidence based upon hearsay.

All witnesses must have first-hand knowledge of matters about which they are testifying. If you say, "Eight mechanics told me the car was no good," the court must ignore that. You are telling them what someone else said. If you bring in one mechanic who says, "I looked at the car and the gears are worn down," then that is good evidence. The witness is telling the court what he saw.

If you bring in a notarized affidavit by a mechanic stating that the gears are worn down, that is no good. The court must ignore it. The reason is that the other side must have a chance to ask your witness questions (cross examination). A person cannot cross examine a piece of paper, so it is usually not good evidence.

There are many exceptions to the hearsay rule, and some hearsay evidence is acceptable. The basis for the exceptions is the reliability of the evidence. Some documents which may be allowed into evidence are certified copies of public records (such as deeds) and business records.

Witness statements of what third parties said are not admissible, but if a person heard an admission by a party to the suit, that is admissible.

Example: If your witness says that he heard a bystander say, "I saw the car run the red light," that is not admissible. The witness did not see anything; you need the bystander in court. But if your witness heard the defendant in the suit say, "I ran the red light," then that is admissible.

WITNESSES

The best evidence you can have is a witness. Parties can be their own witnesses, but disinterested witnesses are better. Before bringing a witness to court, be sure to find out what the witness will say. If there are several witnesses, you want to have the best witness there.

To be sure a witness will appear in court, you can SUBPOENA him or her. (see form 26, p.132.) This is a court order that is delivered by a sheriff commanding a person to appear in court. A PRAECIPE FOR SUBPOENA can be used to request a summons. (see form 25, p.131.) If you want a witness to bring some piece of evidence, you must use a SUBPOENA DUCES TECUM. (see form 27, p.133.) Even if witnesses do not want to come to court they must if you subpoena them. However, you must realize that if people do not want to miss work, and you subpoena them, they may not be your best witness.

Some people, such as relatives or employees, will come at your request and do not have to be subpoenaed. But if you ask someone to come to court and they do not, the trial will go on without their testimony. If you have any doubts that your witnesses will show up, you should subpoena them.

To require witnesses to appear in court, you must pay them a witness fee. This fee is about $7. There is also a fee for mileage, so if they live a long way from the courthouse you will have to pay a few dollars more. For a person who is not a witness to the incident, but who is an expert, you will have to pay them an expert witness fee. This can be whatever they wish to charge (see below). In addition to the witness fee, you will need to pay the sheriff a fee to serve each witness a subpoena. The fee is currently $20.

If you know that a witness will be at the trial to testify for the other side, then you do not have to pay to subpoena him or her. (But remember, if the witness does not show up, you are out of luck.)

As mentioned earlier, it is sometimes possible to have a witness testify by telephone. Ask the judge at your pretrial conference if this may be done in your case.

EXPERT WITNESSES

In some cases, it is important to have an *expert witness*. Often a judge will mention at the pretrial conference that an expert witness is needed. This advice should be heeded. When trying to prove some work was done wrong, it is best to have an expert testify that he examined the work and it was done wrong.

Example: If you are sued for not paying for an air-conditioning repair and you feel the repairman never got it working right, you should bring in another repairman who examined the unit. If you say you fixed it yourself, or your brother-in-law says it wasn't putting out cold air, it won't be as convincing as if you bring in a repairman with twenty years experience who says it obviously did not have enough freon and that he fixed it.

Some judges might allow you to merely bring a receipt for payment for the repairs, but you should ask at the pretrial conference if the judge would prefer better evidence.

You may have to pay an expert to investigate your claim and to appear in court. An expert witness does not have to accept the standard witness fee, but can charge whatever he or she thinks he or she is worth. Some experts charge hundreds of dollars per hour. You should check with a few possible expert witnesses before deciding who to hire. To cut down the expense of having an expert travel to court, ask the judge if he or she may testify by telephone.

ORAL EVIDENCE

It is not true that an agreement must be in writing to win in court. Unless the statute of frauds requires a written agreement, an oral agreement is fully enforceable. The only problem is convincing the judge that there actually was an agreement.

Usually, in a case over an oral agreement either one person will deny that there was an agreement or the parties will disagree over the terms of the agreement. It will be up to the judge to decide which side is telling the truth. Sometimes the judge will find inconsistencies in one side's story, and other times the judge will just have to use his or her gut feeling to decide who is telling the truth.

Occasionally there will be some evidence to support an oral agreement.

Example: If you loaned a friend some money and she paid you $100 a month by check, you could bring copies of the checks from your bank's microfilm records. If she denied there was ever a loan, she will have to come up with a good story about the checks to convince the judge she was not lying. If you cashed the checks at her bank you could subpoena her cancelled checks. If she brought all checks except the ones written to you, you could probably convince the judge that she was hiding something and win the case.

THE PAROL EVIDENCE RULE

Parol evidence is another term for *oral evidence*. The Parol Evidence Rule holds that oral evidence may not be used to contradict a written agreement. An exception to this rule is that when a written agreement is ambiguous then parol evidence may be used to explain what the parties intended.

Example: If a lease says that rent is $500 a month, you cannot expect to win if you tell the judge that the landlord agreed to accept $450. However, if the lease says that the landlord "agrees to take care of the yard before the tenant moves in" then oral testimony could be used to explain what this was suppose to mean.

The importance of this rule is that you must not go to court expecting to win by refuting a written agreement. Find ways in which the other side breached the agreement instead.

PROOF

In criminal law a defendant must be guilty beyond a reasonable doubt. That is a strong burden to overcome. But in civil court a party need only prove his case by a preponderance of the evidence, which means anything over 50% (even 50.0001%). The judge will look at the evidence for each side and will see whose evidence is greater and decide the case accordingly, even if there is some doubt.

COLLECTING YOUR JUDGMENT 8

Once you have won your case, you are only half way to recovery. Next, you must try to collect on your *judgment*. A judgment is only a finding by the court that money is owed. Unfortunately for plaintiffs, debtors' prison has been abolished. A person cannot be put in jail for not paying a judgment. The only thing you can do if a person does not pay a judgment is to look for his or her property and have the sheriff seize it. If a person has no property, your judgment may be worthless.

HEARING IN AID OF EXECUTION

Once you have obtained a judgment against a person you are allowed to force him to bring all of his financial records to court for you and the judge to see. (see form 39, p.146.) This is a session, called a *hearing in aid of execution*, at which the defendant must swear to tell the truth, and you can ask him to list all of his assets and liabilities and show you his deeds and tax returns. This can be time-consuming and embarrassing so a debtor may pay off your judgment to avoid this hearing.

This simple procedure is available to natural persons (not corporations) who handle their case without an attorney. Corporations and attorneys must use another procedure, a *deposition in aid of execution*, which is discussed later in this chapter.

As mentioned in Chapter 6 you can ask that the judgment include an order for the defendant to send you the FACT INFORMATION SHEET. (see form 39, p.146.) If this was done you might be able to start seizing assets without having the hearing. However, if you did not do so, then you can file an EX PARTE MOTION FOR HEARING IN AID OF EXECUTION. (*Ex parte* means that you are making the motion to the judge without previously informing the defendant.) Forms 38 and 39 in this book can be used for this purpose. Because this procedure is relatively new, you will need to ask the judge or clerk how it will be handled in your jurisdiction.

At the hearing, it is important to get information you will need to have to seize assets. This information includes bank account numbers and locations, and vehicle serial numbers. If the defendant says he does not have assets that you think he owns, ask questions about these and try to find out what has been done with them. If money has been taken out of a bank account or if the assets have been given away to a relative or sold cheaply to a friend, you may still be able to seize them. If the defendant appears to be lying to the court under oath, the judge may hold him in contempt.

If you would like to find out if the defendant is lying about his property, or if you are a corporation that cannot use the hearing, you can take several steps to try to find assets. Some places you can check are the following:

1. the county property appraiser's office in the county courthouse for real estate owned by the defendant. (Check other counties if you think they own property elsewhere.) In some counties you can check property records over the Internet;

2. the clerk of the circuit court's official records for more recent information on real estate bought or sold;

3. the Division of Corporations for information on businesses in which the defendant is involved. This will tell you if the defendant is an officer or director of a corporation and if he or she registered a fictitious name. It will not tell you if he or she owns

stock in the business and some people put the stock in their spouse's name. If you know the defendant's spouse's name (ask at the hearing in aid of execution) then you can check if the defendant is running a business under their name;

4. Department of Motor Vehicles for vehicles owned by the defendant. The address is:

    > Department of Motor Vehicles
    > 2900 Apalachee Parkway
    > Tallahassee, FL 32399-0500
    > www.hsmv.state.fl.us/html/contact.html; or,

5. the county tax collector will have records of any boats that the defendant may own.

EXEMPT PROPERTY

Not all property of a debtor may be seized. Florida law exempts much property from seizure, so you must first find out if any property is available. Before taking action to seize a defendant's property you must understand what property is exempt under Florida law. The following property may not be taken in Florida to satisfy a judgment:

- a person's homestead, which may be one-half acre in a municipality or 160 acres of contiguous land outside a municipality;

- wages of the head of a household;

- personal property of up to $1,000.00;

- life insurance proceeds; or,

- disability benefits.

To obtain an exemption, the defendant must meet certain requirements and take action to designate the property exempt. For example, a person who claims his homestead exempt must file an affidavit to that effect or the sheriff will be able to seize and sell it. If you take action against a defendant's property and he does not realize he has the exemption or does not take any action to protect it, you can hold a sale of the property.

Property that is titled in the name of a husband and wife may not be seized by the creditor of only one party. This is why it is important to sue both spouses whenever possible. You cannot seize property owned jointly if you have a judgment against only one owner.

Judgment Lien

The first thing you should do with your judgment is to have it recorded in the official records of the county as a lien against any real property owned by the defendant. When your judgment is signed, it is recorded in the in the official records, but it is not a lien against real property unless a certified copy is recorded. To do this, you must go to the court clerk and have a certified copy prepared for $1.00 per page plus $1.00 for certification. Then, you should have that copy recorded in the official records in each county where the defendant owns property or might own property some day. To do this, use the **Motion for Recordation of Judgment as Lien.** (see form 32, p.138.)

A judgment lien is valid for seven years but can be renewed twice by re-recording within ninety days of the end of the seven years, so that it can remain a lien for up to twenty years. From the time your judgment is signed, it bears interest. The interest rate varies each year and is set by the state comptroller on January 1st. Even if the defendant owns no property now, he may buy some years later or may inherit some. Your $300 judgment today may be a $1600 lien against the defendant's property fifteen years from now. You should keep a note on your calendar (and transfer it to your new calendar each year) to remind yourself to renew your judgment.

NOTE: *The law requires a judgment to have the address of the plaintiff on it in order for it to be a valid lien. Be sure your judgment contains this information before recording it.*

If a person is living in one county, but has family ties or business interests in another, then it would be advisable to file the judgment as a lien in all such counties.

DEPOSITIONS

If the plaintiff is a corporation or is represented by an attorney, the hearing in aid of execution cannot be used. The procedure in such a case is to set up a *deposition* with a court reporter. To set up a deposition you should contact a court reporter and set a date several weeks ahead for the deposition. (Look up "Reporters–Court" in the yellow pages.) The court reporter will explain the costs. Often the fee is $35 to $50 for holding the deposition. If you want it typed up (not usually necessary) it will be a lot more.

Before the deposition you should go to the court clerk and ask that a *Subpoena Duces Tecum* be issued. (see form 27, p.133.) This is a demand to the defendant to bring certain things to the deposition such as deeds, car titles, and tax returns. It will be sent to the sheriff to serve on the defendant. You should take notes while the defendant answers your questions about his or her assets.

When the defendant comes to the deposition, the court reporter will first swear him in. Then you can ask him questions about his assets. (See form 39 for items to ask about.)

If the defendant does not show up for the deposition, you can get a court order that he appear. If that fails, you can have him held in contempt of court. Because this procedure is somewhat complicated, you may wish to use the services of an attorney. If you were entitled to attorney's fees in the original case, it may be possible to have the defendant pay your attorney's fee for this action.

During the deposition, you should ask probing questions that trace all of the defendant's recently-owned assets, as discussed in the previous section. Once you know the defendant's assets, you can start proceedings to have them seized. These are somewhat complicated and should be done by an attorney. But for the adventurous, the procedures are explained below.

LEVY

Ten days after a judgment is rendered, you are allowed to obtain an *execution*. This document can be taken to the sheriff to *levy* upon property of the defendant. Levy means to seize the property and sell it to obtain money to satisfy your judgment.

Before obtaining an execution you should find out from the sheriff if there are any other judgments "docketed" against the defendant prior to yours. If other judgments are prior to yours, then the money from any property seized and sold by the sheriff will first be used to pay the prior judgments. If the amount of prior judgments is not excessive, you should request your judgment to be docketed. The cost is about $10.00. If there are many other judgments docketed, it will probably not be worth your while to start seizing assets that would be used to pay others.

Next, you can ask the sheriff to seize the property and hold a public sale of it. Contact the sheriff for the costs and forms required. The fees for such a service may be several hundred dollars so the property will need to have some value for this procedure to be worthwhile. Before seizing a car or other vehicle you should find out from the Florida Department of Motor Vehicles if there is a lien on it. If so, the lien will have priority over your claim. If the lien is substantial and the defendant has no equity in the vehicle, it would be worthless to seize it. A person who buys the vehicle at the sheriff's sale will have to pay the lien to keep the vehicle.

It is the opinion of some that seizing a nice car, even if there is no equity in it, will be enough of a hassle and embarrassment for the debtor that he will pay you off just to get the car back. You will have to consider your debtor's situation and decide this for yourself.

GARNISHMENT

Garnishment is a procedure for seizing property that is held by a third party to satisfy a judgment. Typical property that can be garnished is a bank account or wages held by an employer which are not exempt. If you know the defendant's bank or employer, you can try garnishment. Do this only if you think there is money in the account or wages owed (Friday morning is usually a good time to garnish wages, Monday is not).

To find out if there is money in a bank account, you can call the bank and say, "I have a check for $500 against account #12345678. Are there sufficient funds to cover it?" If not, call the next day and try a lower amount. Keep in mind, however, that if the account is a joint account with right of survivorship then it usually cannot be garnished for a judgment against only one of the owners.

To begin a garnishment, you must file a MOTION FOR WRIT OF GARNISHMENT. The court clerk may supply a form or you may use Form 33 or 34. The clerk will then issue a Writ of Garnishment and it will be served by the sheriff. The clerk will explain the fees, which include a $100 deposit to cover the attorney's fee of the garnishee.

The Writ of Garnishment asks the garnishee (usually a bank) if it is holding any property of the defendant and if it knows of anyone else making claims to it. After the writ is served, the garnishee must file an answer with the court. If the garnishee fails to answer it may be liable to pay the debt itself! However, to collect in such a case you should consult an attorney.

Within five days after receiving the answer from the garnishee, you must send a NOTICE TO DEFENDANT along with copies of the writ and the garnishee's answer to the defendant and to anyone listed in the answer who might have an interest in the property. (see form 35, p.141.) They then have twenty days to object or assert exemptions. You must file a copy of this notice with the court certifying that it has been sent.

If there is any objection to the garnishment, a trial will need to be held and you will probably need the services of an attorney. If the garnishee files an answer admitting it holds property and there are no issues to resolve, you can file an ACCEPTANCE OF GARNISHEE'S ANSWER AND MOTION FOR FINAL JUDGMENT (form 36) along with a FINAL JUDGMENT APPROVING GARNISHMENT (form 37).

If wages are being garnished, there are both state and federal limitations. Under Florida Statutes, Section 222.11 the wages of the head of a family cannot be garnished if they are under $500 a week. If they are over $500 a week they can only be garnished if the person has agreed in writing. If the wages have been deposited in an account, they cannot be garnished for six months. After six months they can be.

WAGES Under the federal Consumer Credit Protection Act, you can only garnish the following amounts of net income (after tax withholdings, social security and medicare):

1. If paid weekly:

    Nothing on the first $100.50
    All of the amount between $100.50 and $134.00
    25% of the amount above $134.00

2. If paid bi-weekly:

    Nothing on the first $201.00
    All of the amount between $201.00 and $268.00
    25% of the amount above $268.00

3. If paid semi-monthly:

    Nothing on the first $217.75
    All of the amount between $217.75 and $290.33
    25% of the amount above $290.33

4. If paid monthly:

    Nothing on the first $435.50
    All of the amount between $435.50 and $580.67
    25% of the amount above $580.67 (United States Code, Title 15, Section 1673.)

BANKRUPTCY

If the defendant files bankruptcy, all legal actions must immediately stop. You can be held in contempt of federal court if you take any action to further your case or acquire the defendant's property. If the defendant files liquidation bankruptcy then your claim is wiped out and you are forever barred from collecting on it. If the defendant files reorganization bankruptcy, you may be paid at a later time in full or in part. If a bankruptcy is withdrawn before the debtor is discharged, you may proceed with your claim.

You may receive a paper called a *suggestion of bankruptcy* informing you that the defendant has filed. However, even if you do not receive this, but are only verbally told that bankruptcy has been filed, you should stop all collection efforts and check with the bankruptcy court.

Even if you quickly seize assets before bankruptcy, it will not help you because the bankruptcy court can order you to return any money or property you received within ninety days of the filing.

If the defendant filed bankruptcy, you should receive a notice from the bankruptcy court notifying you of how much time you have to file a *proof of claim*. Some courts will send you a form to fill out, but others expect you to provide your own form. One is included in this book as form 45 p.153.

SATISFACTION OF JUDGMENT

If a defendant pays off your judgment, you must file notice with the court that it has been paid. To do so, use the SATISFACTION OF JUDGMENT form. (see form 41, p.149.)

Rehearings and Appeals 9

If you lose your small claims case, you sometimes have the right to a second chance. However, these cases are limited. This chapter explains when and how you can have a second chance.

Vacating a Default

If you do not show up for the pretrial conference or for the trial, a default and a judgment may be entered against you. If you have a good excuse, you may be able to have the default and judgment set aside and a new hearing or trial set. Besides a good excuse for missing the court date, you will also need to provide evidence that you have a good defense and a good chance of winning the case. If it looks like you would lose at trial anyway, the judge will see no reason to set a new trial. To ask that the default against you be set aside, use the MOTION TO SET ASIDE DEFAULT AND DEFAULT JUDGMENT. (see form 31, p.137.)

Appeal

After losing a hard-fought case, a person's first reaction is to promise an appeal. However, one must realize that appeals are expensive and rarely successful.

When a trial court hears a case, it decides questions of fact and questions of law. Usually the questions of fact are most important: Were the repairs done correctly? Was the bill paid in cash? Was a notice mailed to the tenant? Questions of law concern the legal rights of the parties under those facts.

Questions of fact are never appealable. An appeals court can only review the legal decision of the judge, which is not often wrong. If the judge didn't believe you did a good repair job or didn't believe one of your witnesses, you don't get a second chance to convince an appeals court or to bring more witnesses. The appeals court will only review the legal decision of the judge and accept all of his fact findings. Only if the judge made an obvious legal mistake will the judgment be overturned.

Our legal system is not perfect. Sometimes liars win and there is no way to reverse the decision. The best you can do is be prepared for your trial with all the evidence at your disposal.

COURT
REPORTER

Another obstacle to an appeal is that it is often important to have a court reporter's transcript of the trial. This means you must hire a court reporter to attend the trial and type out every word said. It is very expensive and must be arranged ahead of time. If you want to win at any cost and guarantee your right to appeal, then you can hire a court reporter to attend the trial. This may cost $35 or $50 if it does not last long and if you do not ask that the transcript be typed. At the end of the hearing, tell the court reporter not to type the transcript unless you contact him or her.

If the law is on your side in a case but the judge seems to be more sympathetic to the other side at the pretrial conference, you might want to hire a court reporter to transcribe the hearing just to let the judge know that you will appeal if he or she does not follow the law.

NOTICE OF
APPEAL

If you feel the judge made an error of law in deciding your case, you can file a **NOTICE OF APPEAL** within thirty days of the judgment. (see form 42, p.150.) This is a simple statement that you are appealing the case to the circuit court. After you file the notice, the procedure will usually be as follows:

1. within fifty days of the filing of the notice, the clerk will prepare a record of your case;

2. within seventy days of the filing of the notice the parties should prepare and submit a "brief" to the court. A brief is a legal memorandum of the law as it applies to the case; and,

3. within 110 days of the filing of the notice the clerk will forward the file to the circuit court.

The court may make its ruling merely on the briefs of the parties or there may be oral argument. In either case, the only thing the court is concerned with is the law and no new evidence may be presented. For more information on the appellate process, check the Florida Rules of Appellate Procedure at any law library.

REHEARING OR NEW TRIAL

One alternative to an appeal is to request a rehearing or a new trial. (A *rehearing* is requested when there was no jury at the original proceeding and a *new trial* is requested where there was a jury.)

In some cases, such as when new evidence is discovered, when evidence is found to be false, or when an important law was overlooked by the judge, a rehearing may be granted. But it is rarely successful except in extreme cases.

To request a rehearing or new trial, you must file a MOTION FOR REHEARING or a MOTION FOR NEW TRIAL within ten days of the entry of the judgment or the jury verdict. The motion should state that you are asking for a rehearing or a new trial and state with particularity what the grounds are. You should make your best case in this motion and not save any surprises for the hearing since you might not get one.

DEADLINES

Appeals must be filed within thirty days of the judgment and requests for rehearings within ten days. Both procedures can be complicated and it is usually advantageous to seek the advice of an attorney.

CROSS APPEAL

If your opponent appeals the verdict in your case, you should consider appealing as well. If both sides are asking for more, there is a greater chance of a settlement or a compromise verdict than if only one side is asking for something. If you did not get everything you were asking for in your case, you can *cross appeal* and ask for what you originally sought. To do so, use the NOTICE OF CROSS APPEAL. (see form 43, p.151.)

GLOSSARY

A

alias service. A second attempt to serve papers on a party.

answer. A paper filed by a party in response to a legal pleading.

arbitration. Negotiations in which an arbitrator listens to both side of a dispute and makes a decision as to who shall prevail.

C

claim. A formal request for compensation from another party.

cost bond. A guarantee by an insurance company to pay the costs of the defendant if he or she wins.

counter-defendant. Name given to plaintiff if the original defendant files a counterclaim.

counter-plaintiff. Name given to defendant if he or she files a counterclaim.

counterclaim. When a defendant sues a plaintiff after being sued by the plaintiff, he or she files a counterclaim.

crossclaim. When there are two or more defendants and one defendant sues another defendant in the same suit, he files a crossclaim against the other defendant.

D

damages. Financial measure of harm done to a person.

default. Entry made by a court against a party who fails to show up, usually entitling the other side to win the case.

defendant. The person contesting against a claim.

deposition. The asking of questions of a party to a suit under oath.

duress. Pressure that compels a person to do something they would not ordinarily do.

E

expert witness. A person asked to testify in court, not because of familiarity with the case, but because of expert knowledge in some aspect of the case.

G

garnishment. The seizure of some money or property through court action.

grounds. Legal basis for doing something.

H

hearsay. Evidence based upon what is heard rather than actual experience.

I

implied warranty. A warranty enforced by a court based not on any explicit statements of a party but on his or her acts or related claims.

J

judgment. A final order by a court deciding a case.

L

lemon law. A law giving remedies for the sale of a defective automobile.

liability. Being made legally responsible to pay for something.

M

malpractice. Providing professional services that are below the legally required standard of care.

mediation. Negotiations in which a negotiator attempts to help each side see the other's viewpoint and come to a mutual settlement.

motion. A request for a court to take specific action.

N

negligence. Failure to exercise the care that the law requires.

P

parol evidence rule. Rule that oral evidence may not be used to contradict written evidence.

piercing the corporate veil. Holding owners of a corporation responsible for the corporation's obligations..

plaintiff. The person filing a claim.

pleading. A document telling the court what the legal claim is and what outcome is sought.

pluries service. A third or subsequent attempt to serve papers on a person.

promissory note. A written promise to pay a sum of money.

Q

quantum meruit. Recovery based on the value of a service rather than an agreement to pay.

R

reformation. The rewriting of a contract by a court to make it more equitable.

registered agent. The person authorized by a corporation to receive legal papers for it.

replevin. A suit for return of property.

rescission. Canceling a contract and putting the parties back in their original pre-contract positions.

restitution. Paying back another's losses.

S

service of process. The act of handing court papers to a party in the case.

specific performance. A court order requiring a party to do exactly what a contract calls for.

statute of frauds. Law requiring an agreement to be in writing.

statute of limitations. Law saying how long after an event a lawsuit can be filed.

subpoena duces tecum. A document issued by the court ordering a person to bring something to a hearing.

subpoena. A document issued by the court ordering a person to appear at a hearing.

summons. A court document informing someone of a proceeding against him or her and requiring him or her to respond.

T

third party defendant. When a defendant wants to bring another party into the suit that party is the third party defendant.

U

usury. An unlawful rate of interest.

V

venue. The correct court in which a suit should be filed.

W

waiver. Giving up a legal right.

warranty of fitness. A guaranty that an item will perform the purpose for which it was sold.

warranty of merchantability. A guaranty that an item will perform what it was made to do.

warranty of title. A guaranty that a buyer is receiving ownership rights to the thing he or she is buying.

APPENDIX A
LAWYER REFERRAL SERVICES

The following pages contain a list of lawyer referral offices. The best way to find a good lawyer is to use one who has been recommended by a friend or relative. If these people cannot recommend one, the lawyer referral service can be helpful.

The lawyer referral service will allow you a short consultation with a lawyer for a small fee. Since you are paying a fee you should obtain some useful legal advice about your case. Ask the lawyer what are the strong and weak points of your case and what evidence would be most useful.

Lawyer Referral Offices

Broward County Bar Association
1051 S.E. Third Ave.
Ft. Lauderdale, FL 33316
954-764-8310

Clearwater Bar Association
(North Pinellas County)
314 S. Missouri Ave., Suite 107
Clearwater, FL 33756
727-461-4880

Collier County Bar Association
3301 E. Tamiami Trail, Bldg. L, Fifth Floor
Naples, FL 34112
941-775-8566
941-775-3939

Escambia-Santa Rosa Bar Association
30 W. Government St.
Pensacola, FL 32501
850-434-6009

Hillsborough County Bar Association
101 East Kennedy Blvd., Suite 2110
Tampa, FL 33602
813-221-7780

Jacksonville Bar Association
(Baker, Clay, Duval, Nassau)
1301 Riverplace Blvd., Suite 730
Jacksonville, FL 32207
904-399-5780

Orange County Bar Association
880 N. Orange Ave., Suite 100
Orlando, FL 32801
407-422-4537

Palm Beach County Bar Association
1601 Belvedere Road, Suite 302 East
West Palm Beach, FL 33406
561-687-3266
(North Palm Bch.)
561-451-3256
(South Palm Bch.)

St. Petersburg Bar Association
(South Pinellas County)
2600 Dr. M. L. King Street North, Suite 602
P.O. Box 7538
St. Petersburg, FL 33734-7538
727-821-5450

Tallahassee Bar Association
(Leon, Jefferson, Wakulla, Gadsden,
Liberty, Franklin)
P.O. Box 813
Tallahassee, Florida 32302
850-681-0601

West Pasco Bar Association
7529 Redcoat Ave.
Port Richey, FL 34668-2941
727-848-7433

All other counties contact:
The **Florida** Bar Lawyer Referral Service
The Florida Bar
650 Apalachee Parkway
Tallahassee, FL 32399-2300
800-342-8011
850-561-5844

APPENDIX B
FLORIDA
SMALL CLAIMS RULES

This appendix includes most of the official Florida Small Claims Rules that govern actions in Small Claims Court. There are other rules (7.300–7.345) that are sample forms, but these have been omitted since we include an extensive set of forms in Appendix D.

Rule 7.110.   Dismissal of Actions

Rule 7.130.   Continuances and Settlements

Rule 7.135.   Summary Disposition

Rule 7.140.   Trial

Rule 7.150.   Jury Trials

Rule 7.160.   Failure of Plaintiff or Both Parties to Appear

Rule 7.170.   Default; Judgment

Rule 7.180.   Motions for New Trial; Time for; Contents

Rule 7.190.   Relief from Judgment or Order; Clerical Mistakes

Rule 7.200.   Executions

Rule 7.210.   Stay of Judgment and Execution

Rule 7.220.   Supplementary Proceedings

Rule 7.221.   Hearing in Aid of Execution

Rule 7.230.   Appellate Review

RULE 7.010. TITLE AND SCOPE

(a) Title. These rules shall be cited as Florida Small Claims Rules and may be abbreviated "Fla.Sm.Cl.R." These rules shall be construed to implement the simple, speedy, and inexpensive trial of actions at law in county courts.

(b) Scope. These rules are applicable to all actions at law of a civil nature in the county courts in which the demand or value of property involved does not exceed $5,000 exclusive of costs, interest, and attorneys' fees; if there is a difference between the time period prescribed by these rules and section 51.011, Florida Statutes, the statutory provision shall govern.

Committee Notes

1978 Amendment. The addition to (b) is designed to eliminate confusion caused by denomination of Section 51.011, Florida Statutes, as "Summary Procedure."

RULE 7.020. APPLICABILITY OF RULES OF CIVIL PROCEDURE

(a) Generally. Florida Rules of Civil Procedure 1.090(a), (b), and (c); 1.190(e); 1.210(b); 1.260; 1.410; and 1.560 are applicable in all actions covered by these rules.

(b) Discovery. Any party represented by an attorney is subject to discovery pursuant to Florida Rules of Civil Procedure 1.280-1.380 directed at said party, without order of court. If a party proceeding without an attorney directs discovery to a party represented by an attorney, the represented party may also use discovery pursuant to the above-mentioned rules without leave of court. When a party is unrepresented and has not initiated discovery pursuant to Florida Rules of Civil Procedure 1.280-1.380, the opposing party shall not be entitled to initiate such discovery without leave of court. However, the time for such discovery procedures may be prescribed by the court.

(c) Additional Rules. In any particular action, the court may order that action to proceed under 1 or more additional Florida Rules of Civil Procedure on application of any party or the stipulation of all parties on the court's own motion.

Committee Notes

1972 Amendment. Subdivision (a) is amended by giving the court authority to apply additional rules of civil procedure in any particular case on the application of a party, stipulation of all parties, or order on the court's own motion.

1978 Amendment. These proposed amendments would help prevent overreaching and the ability of one party to obtain judgment without giving the court the full opportunity to consider the merits of the case. When attorneys are involved, the rule would preserve the ability of the parties to fully develop their cases.

1996 Amendment. The addition of Fla. R. Civ. P. 1.380 enables the court to issue and impose sanctions for failure to comply with discovery requests.

RULE 7.040. CLERICAL AND ADMINISTRATIVE DUTIES OF CLERK

(a) Generally. The clerk of the circuit court or the clerk of the county court in those counties where such a clerk is provided (hereinafter referred to as the clerk) shall:

(1) maintain a trial calendar. The placing of any action thereon with the date and time of trial is notice to all concerned of the order in which they may expect such action to be called;

(2) maintain a docket book and a judgment book (which may be the same book) in which accurate entries of all actions brought before the court and notations of the proceedings shall be made including the date of filing; the date of issuance, service, and return of process; the appearance of such parties as may appear; the fact of trial, whether by court or jury; the issuance of execution and to whom issued and the date thereof and return thereon and, when satisfied, a marginal entry of the date thereof; the issuance of a certified copy; a memorandum of the items of costs including witness fees; and the record of the verdict of the jury or finding of the judge, and the judgment, including damages and costs, which judgments may be kept in a separate judgment book; and

(3) maintain an alphabetical index by parties' names with reference to action and case number.

(b) Minute Book. It shall not be necessary for the clerk to maintain a minute book for small claims.

Court Commentary

1972 Amendment. See also rule 7.050(c).

RULE 7.050. COMMENCEMENT OF ACTION; STATEMENT OF CLAIM

(a) Commencement.

(1) *Statement of Claim.* Actions are commenced by the filing of a statement of claim in concise form, which shall inform the defendant of the basis and the amount of the claim. If the claim is based on a written document, a copy or the material part thereof shall be attached to the statement of claim.

(2) *Party Not Represented by Attorney to Sign.* A party, individual, or corporation who or which has no attorney handling such cause shall sign that party's statement of claim or other paper and state that party's address and telephone number, including area code. However, if the trial court in its discretion determines that the plaintiff is engaged in the business of collecting claims and holds such claim being sued upon by purchase, assignment, or management arrangement in the operation of such business, the court may require that corporation to provide counsel in the prosecution of the cause. A corporation may be represented at any stage of the trial court proceedings by an officer of the corporation or any employee authorized by an officer of the corporation.

(b) Parties. The names, addresses, and telephone numbers, including area code, of all parties or their attorneys, if any, must be stated on the statement of claim. Additionally, attorneys shall include their Florida Bar number on all papers filed with the court.

(c) Clerk's Duties. The clerk shall assist in the preparation of a statement of claim and other papers to be filed in the action at the request of any litigant. The clerk shall not be required to prepare papers on constructive service, substituted service, proceedings supplementary to execution, or discovery procedures.

(d) Memorandum on Hearing Date. The court shall furnish all parties with a memorandum of the day and hour set for the hearing.

(e) Replevin. In those replevin cases to which these rules are applicable, the clerk of the county court shall set the hearing required by section 78.065(2)(a), Florida Statutes (prejudgment replevin order to show cause hearings) and rule 7.050(d) (pretrial conferences) at the same time.

Committee Notes

1988 Amendment. Subdivision (a)(2): To clarify who may appear and represent a corporation in a small claims case.

Subdivision (b): First sentence is to conform Florida Small Claims Rules with Florida Rules of Judicial Administration 2.060(d) and 2.060(e). Second sentence is to conform to proposed amendment to rules of judicial administration.

Subdivision (e): Require that the order to show cause hearing required in small claims replevin cases and the pretrial conference required by the small claims rules be held at the same time to save time and avoid confusion.

RULE 7.060. PROCESS AND VENUE

(a) Summons Required. A summons entitled Notice to Appear stating the time and place of hearing shall be served on the defendant. The summons or notice to appear shall inform the defendant, in a separate paragraph containing bold type, of the defendant's right of venue. This paragraph on venue shall read:

Right to Venue. The law gives the person or company who has sued you the right to file suit in any one of several places as listed below. However, if you have been sued in any place other than one of these places, you, as the defendant, have the right to request that the case be moved to a proper location or venue. A proper location or venue may be one of the following:

1. Where the contract was entered into.

2. If the suit is on an unsecured promissory note, where the note is signed or where the maker resides.

3. If the suit is to recover property or to foreclose a lien, where the property is located.

4. Where the event giving rise to the suit occurred.

5. Where any one or more of the defendants sued reside.

6. Any location agreed to in a contract.

7. In an action for money due, if there is no agreement as to where suit may be filed, where payment is to be made.

If you, as a defendant, believe the plaintiff has not sued in one of these correct places, you must appear on your court date and orally request a transfer or you must file a written request for transfer in affidavit form (sworn to under oath) with the court 7 days prior to your first court date and send a copy to the plaintiff or plaintiff's attorney, if any.

(b) Copy of Claim to Be Served. A copy of the statement of claim shall be served with the

summons/notice to appear.

Committee Notes

1988 Amendment. A statement is added to the "right to venue notice" on the summons/notice to appear that proper venue also lies in the county where payment is to be made. This conforms with Florida law.

Clarification has been made that the notice is now known as the summons/notice to appear.

Court Commentary

1980 Amendment. If the statutory venue, chapter 47, Florida Statutes, is changed by the legislature, this change should be reflected in the required notice.

RULE 7.070. METHOD OF SERVICE OF PROCESS

Service of process shall be effected as provided by law or as provided by Florida Rules of Civil Procedure 1.070(a)-(h). Constructive service or substituted service of process may be effected as provided by law. Service of process on Florida residents only may also be effected by certified mail, return receipt signed by the defendant, or someone

authorized to receive mail at the residence or principal place of business of the defendant. Either the clerk or an attorney of record may mail the certified mail, the cost of which is in addition to the filing fee.

Committee Notes

1978 Amendment. Present rule provides for certified or registered mail. Certified mail has not been satisfactory since the Postal Service does not deliver to the defendant in all cases.

1984 Amendment. Mail service is allowed on persons authorized to receive mail for the defendant similar to substituted service by the sheriff on a resident of the defendant's abode. The proposal clarifies the rule that service by mail is not available for out-of-state defendants.

1992 Amendment. The committee has found that most jurisdictions forward the summons and complaint for service by certified mail rather than registered mail. Therefore, the rule is changed to conform to the custom and to be more in keeping with the other service requirements that are required by certified mail as opposed to registered mail.

1996 Amendment. The rule is being modified to exclude Fla. R. Civ. P. 1.070(i) because Small Claims Rule 7.110(e) provides for dismissal of a claim for failure to prosecute after 6 months of inactivity.

Court Commentary

1972 Amendment. The payment of costs of service by certified or registered mail from the filing fee is authorized by section 34.041(1), Florida Statutes; chapter 72-404, Laws of Florida.

RULE 7.080. SERVICE OF PLEADINGS AND PAPERS OTHER THAN STATEMENT OF CLAIM

(a) When Required. Copies of all pleadings and papers subsequent to the notice to appear, except applications for witness subpoenas and orders and judgments entered in open court, shall be served on each party. One against whom a default has been entered is entitled to be served only with pleadings asserting new or additional claims.

(b) How Made. When a party is represented by an attorney, service of papers other than the statement of claim and notice to appear shall be made on the attorney unless the court orders service to be made on the party. Service shall be made by delivering the paper to the party or the party's attorney, as the case may be, or by mailing it to the party's last known address.

(c) Filing. All original pleadings and papers shall be filed with the court either before service or immediately thereafter. The court may allow a copy to be substituted for the original of any document.

(d) Filing with the Court Defined. The filing of papers with the court as required by these rules is made by filing them with the clerk, except that the judge may permit the papers to be filed with the judge, in which event the judge shall note thereon the filing date and transmit them to the clerk, and the clerk shall file them as of the same date they were filed with the judge.

(e) Certificate of Service.

(1) When any party or attorney in substance certifies:

"I certify that a copy hereof has been furnished to (here insert name or names) by (delivery) (mail) on ....(date)......

Party or party's attorney"

the certificate is prima facie proof of such service in compliance with all rules of court and law.

(2) When any paper is served by the clerk, a docket entry shall be made showing the mode and date of service. Such entry is sufficient proof of service without a separate certificate of service.

(f) When Unrepresented Party Fails to Show Service. If a party who is not represented by an attorney files a paper that does not show service of a copy on all other parties, the clerk shall serve a copy of it on all other parties.

Court Commentary

1972 Amendment. Subdivisions (a), (b), (c), (d), and (e) are substantially the same as Florida Rule of Civil Procedure 1.080(a), (b), (d), (e), and (f).

RULE 7.090. APPEARANCE; DEFENSIVE PLEADINGS; TRIAL DATE

(a) Appearance. On the date and time appointed in the notice to appear, the plaintiff and defendant shall appear personally or by counsel.

(b) Notice to Appear; Pretrial Conference. The summons/notice to appear shall specify that the initial appearance shall be for a pretrial conference. The initial pretrial conference shall be set by the clerk not more than 35 days from the date of the filing of the action. At the pretrial conference, all of the following matters shall be considered:

(1) The simplification of issues.

(2) The necessity or desirability of amendments to the pleadings.

(3) The possibility of obtaining admissions of fact and of documents that avoid unnecessary proof.

(4) The limitations on the number of witnesses.

(5) The possibilities of settlement.

(6) Such other matters as the court in its discretion deems necessary.

Form 7.322 shall and form 7.323 may be used in conjunction with this rule.

(c) Defensive Pleadings. Unless required by order of court, written pretrial motions and defensive pleadings are not necessary. If filed, copies of such pleadings shall be served on all other parties to the action at or prior to the pretrial conference or within such time as the court may designate. The filing of a motion or a defensive pleading shall not excuse the personal appearance of a party or attorney on the initial appearance date (pretrial conference).

(d) Trial Date. The court shall set the case for trial not more than 60 days from the date of the pretrial conference. At least 10 days' notice of the time of trial shall be given. The parties may stipulate to a shorter or longer time for setting trial with the approval of the court. This rule does not apply to actions to which chapter 51, Florida Statutes, applies.

(e) Waiver of Appearance at Pretrial Conference. Where all parties are represented by an attorney, counsel may agree to waive personal appearance at the initial pretrial conference, if a written agreement of waiver signed by all attorneys is presented to the court prior to or at the pretrial conference. The agreement shall contain a short statement of the disputed issues of fact and law, the number of witnesses expected to testify, an estimate of the time needed to try the case, and any stipulations of fact. The court shall forthwith set the case for trial within the time prescribed by these rules.

(f) Appearance at Mediation. In small claims actions, an attorney may appear on behalf of a party at mediation if the attorney has full authority to settle without further consultation. Unless otherwise ordered by the court, a nonlawyer representative may appear on behalf of a party to a small claims mediation if the representative has the party's signed written authority to appear and has full authority to settle without further consultation. In either event, the party need not appear in person.

(g) Agreement. Any agreements reached as a fesult of small claims mediation shall be written by the form of a stipulation. The stipulation may be entered as an order of the court.

Committee Notes

1972 Amendment. Rule 7.120 is incorporated in subdivision (c). It is slightly expanded to provide for a computation period from service by mail and to give the parties the right to stipulate to a shorter time for the trial.

1984 Amendment. This change requires the use of a pretrial procedure and requires both parties to attend the pretrial conference which can be used to resolve pretrial motions. The use of a pretrial previously varied from county to county.

1988 Amendment. (b) 1st sentence—Chair's clarification.

2nd sentence—Require the clerk to set the initial pretrial conference within a reasonable time after fil-

ing of the action taking into consideration the fact that the time standards guideline for small claims cases is 95 days.

3rd sentence—State within the small claims rules what matters shall be considered at the pretrial conference rather than by reference to Florida Rule of Civil Procedure 1.220(a), which has been amended several times and is generally not applicable to small claims cases.

4th sentence—Direct that new form 7.322 shall and that new form 7.323 may be used statewide.

(c) Clarifies that a personal appearance is required at the pretrial conference when a defense motion is filed.

(e) Adds a provision for waiving counsel's appearance at the pretrial conference where all parties are represented by counsel.

RULE 7.100. COUNTERCLAIMS, SETOFFS, THIRD-PARTY COMPLAINTS, TRANSFER WHEN JURISDICTION EXCEEDED

(a) Compulsory Counterclaim. Any claim of the defendant against the plaintiff, arising out of the same transaction or occurrence which is the subject matter of the plaintiff's claim, shall be filed not less than 5 days prior to the initial appearance date (pretrial conference) or within such time as the court designates or it is deemed to be abandoned.

(b) Permissive Counterclaim. Any claim or setoff of the defendant against the plaintiff, not arising out of the transaction or occurrence which is the subject matter of the plaintiff's claim, may be filed not less than 5 days before the initial appearance date (pretrial conference) or within such time as the court designates, and tried, providing that such permissive claim is within the jurisdiction of the court.

(c) How Filed. Counterclaims and setoffs shall be filed in writing. If additional time is needed to prepare a defense, the court may continue the action.

(d) Transfer When Beyond Jurisdiction. When a counterclaim or setoff exceeds the jurisdiction of the court, it shall be filed in writing before or at the hearing, and the action shall then be transferred to the court having jurisdiction thereof. As evidence of good faith, the counterclaimant shall deposit a sum sufficient to pay the filing fee in the court to which the case is to be transferred with the counterclaim, which shall be sent with the record to the court to which transferred. Failure to make the deposit waives the right to transfer.

(e) Third-Party Complaints. A defendant may cause a statement of claim to be served on a person not a party to the action who is or may be liable to the defendant for all or part of the plaintiff's claim against the defendant. A defendant must obtain leave of court on motion made at the initial pretrial conference and must file the third-party complaint within such time as the court may allow. The clerk shall schedule a supplemental pretrial conference, and on the date and time appointed in the notice to appear the third-party plaintiff and the third-party defendant shall appear personally or by counsel. If additional time is needed for the third-party defendant to prepare a defense, the court may continue the action. Any party may move to strike the third-party claim or for its severance or separate trial. When a counterclaim is asserted against the plaintiff, the plaintiff may bring in a third-party defendant under circumstances that would entitle a defendant to do so under this rule.

Committee Notes

1988 Amendment. Provides for and authorizes third-party claims so that all issues may be addressed and resolved. Also provides for a title change.

RULE 7.110. DISMISSAL OF ACTIONS

(a) Voluntary Dismissal; Effect Thereof.

(1) *By Parties.* Except in actions where property has been seized or is in the custody of the court, an action may be dismissed by the plaintiff without order of court (A) by the plaintiff informing the defendant and clerk of the dismissal before the trial date fixed in the notice to appear, or before retirement of the jury in a case tried before a jury or before submission of a nonjury case to the court for decision, or (B) by filing a stipulation of dismissal signed by all parties who have appeared in the action. Unless otherwise stated, the dismissal is without prejudice, except that a dismissal operates as an adjudication on the merits when a plaintiff has

once dismissed in any court an action based on or including the same claim.

(2) *By Order of the Court; If Counterclaim.* Except as provided in subdivision (a)(1) of this rule, an action shall not be dismissed at a party's instance except upon order of the court and on such terms and conditions as the court deems proper. If a counterclaim has been made by the defendant before the plaintiff dismisses voluntarily, the action shall not be dismissed against the defendant's objections unless the counterclaim can remain pending for independent adjudication. Unless otherwise specified in the order, a dismissal under this subdivision is without prejudice.

(b) Involuntary Dismissal. Any party may move for dismissal of an action or of any claim against that party for failure of an adverse party to comply with these rules or any order of court. After a party seeking affirmative relief in an action has completed the presentation of evidence, any other party may move for a dismissal on the ground that upon the facts and the law the party seeking affirmative relief has shown no right to relief without waiving the right to offer evidence in the event the motion is not granted. The court may then determine them and render judgment against the party seeking affirmative relief or may decline to render any judgment until the close of all the evidence. Unless the court in its order for dismissal otherwise specifies, a dismissal under this subdivision and any dismissal not provided for in this rule, other than a dismissal for lack of jurisdiction or for improper venue or for lack of an indispensable party, operates as an adjudication on the merits.

(c) Dismissal of Counterclaim. The provisions of this rule apply to the dismissal of any counterclaim.

(d) Costs. Costs in any action dismissed under this rule shall be assessed and judgment for costs entered in that action. If a party who has once dismissed a claim in any court of this state commences an action based on or including the same claim against the same adverse party, the court shall make such order for the payment of costs of the claim previously dismissed as it may deem proper and shall stay the proceedings in the action until the party seeking affirmative relief has complied with the order.

(e) Failure to Prosecute. All actions in which it affirmatively appears that no action has been taken by filing of pleadings, order of court, or otherwise for a period of 6 months shall be dismissed by the court on its own motion or on motion of any interested person, whether a party to the action or not, after 30 days' notice to the parties, unless a stipulation staying the action has been filed with the court, or a stay order has been filed, or a party shows good cause in writing at least 5 days before the hearing on the motion why the action should remain pending.

Committee Notes

1978 Amendment. Former subdivision (e) provided for 1 year rather than 6 months.

1984 Amendment. Subdivision (e) is changed to allow more time for an attorney to inquire about the status of a claim. Many actions are disposed of by a stipulation to pay, and it may take longer than 10 days to determine the amount due, if any.

1996 Amendment. Subdivision (e) is amended to be consistent with Fla. R. Civ. P. 1.420(e), which includes specific language concerning a stipulation staying the action approved by the court or a stay order as a condition when an action would not automatically be up for dismissal based on lack of prosecution.

Court Commentary

1972 Amendment. Substantially the same as Florida Rule of Civil Procedure 1.420.

RULE 7.130. CONTINUANCES AND SETTLEMENTS

(a) Continuances. A continuance may be granted only upon good cause shown. The motion for continuance may be oral, but the court may require that it be reduced to writing. The action shall be set again for trial as soon as practicable and the parties shall be given timely notice.

(b) Settlements. Settlements in full or by installment payments made by the parties out of the presence of the court are encouraged. The plaintiff shall notify the clerk of settlement, and the case may be dismissed or continued pending payments. Upon failure of a party to perform the terms of any stipulation or agreement for settlement of the claim before judgment, the court may enter appropriate

judgment without notice upon the creditor's filing of an affidavit of the amount due.

Committee Notes

1984 Amendment. Subdivision (b) is altered to conform with rule 7.210(c), which provides for an affidavit but no notice.

RULE 7.135. SUMMARY DISPOSITION

At pretrial conference or at any subsequent hearing, if there is no triable issue, the court shall summarily enter an appropriate order or judgment.

RULE 7.140. TRIAL

(a) Time. The trial date shall be set by the court at pretrial.

(b) Determination. Issues shall be settled and motions determined summarily.

(c) Pretrial. The pretrial conference should narrow contested factual issues. The case may proceed to trial with the consent of both parties.

(d) Settlement. At any time before judgment, the judge shall make an effort to assist the parties in settling the controversy by conciliation or compromise.

(e) Unrepresented Parties. In an effort to further the proceedings and in the interest of securing substantial justice, the court shall assist any party not represented by an attorney on:

(1) courtroom decorum; and

(2) order of presentation of material evidence.

The court may not instruct any party not represented by an attorney on accepted rules of law. The court shall not act as an advocate for a party.

(f) How Conducted. The trial may be conducted informally but with decorum befitting a court of justice. The rules of evidence applicable to trial of civil actions apply but are to be liberally construed. At the discretion of the court, testimony of any party or witness may be presented over the telephone. Additionally, at the discretion of the court an attorney may represent a party or witness over the telephone without being physically present before the court.

Committee Notes

1984 Amendment. (a) Changed to conform this rule with the requirement for pretrials.

(c) Allows the cases to proceed to trial with consent of the parties.

(f) This is similar to the proposed amendment to the Florida Rules of Civil Procedure to allow depositions by telephone. Since the court has discretion to allow this testimony, all procedural safeguards could be maintained by the court. Since the court is also the trier of fact, the testimony could be rejected if unreliable.

1988 Amendment. Extends the taking of testimony over the telephone to include parties, deletes the agreement of the parties provision, and adds authorization for an attorney to represent a party or witness over the telephone without being physically present before the court.

1996 Amendment. The revised version of subdivision (e) addresses the need to expressly provide that the judge, while able to assist an unrepresented party, should not act as an advocate for that party.

RULE 7.150. JURY TRIALS

Jury trials may be had upon written demand of the plaintiff at the time of the commencement of the suit, or by the defendant within 5 days after service of notice of suit or at the pretrial conference, if any. Otherwise jury trial shall be deemed waived.

Committee Notes

1984 Amendment. The purpose of the cost deposit formerly required was to discourage frivolous demands for jury trials. The committee feels that there should be no distinction between the taxation of costs in a $300 claim and a $3,000 claim.

RULE 7.160. FAILURE OF PLAINTIFF OR BOTH PARTIES TO APPEAR

(a) Plaintiff. If plaintiff fails to appear on the initial appearance date (pretrial conference), or fails to appear at trial, the action may be dismissed for want of prosecution, defendant may proceed to trial on the merits, or the action may be continued as the judge may direct.

(b) Both Parties. If both parties fail to appear, the judge may continue the action or dismiss it for want of prosecution at that time or later as justice requires.

RULE 7.170. DEFAULT; JUDGMENT

(a) Default. If the defendant does not appear at the scheduled time, the plaintiff is entitled to a default to be entered by either the judge or clerk.

(b) Final Judgment. After default is entered, the judge shall receive evidence establishing the damages and enter judgment in accordance with the evidence and the law. The judge may inquire into and prevent abuses of venue prior to entering judgment.

Court Commentary

1972 Amendment. Evidence may be by testimony, affidavit, or other competent means.

1980 Amendment. By the amendment to this rule, the judge is permitted to ensure by any means which the judge deems appropriate that venue is not being abused.

RULE 7.180. MOTIONS FOR NEW TRIAL; TIME FOR; CONTENTS

(a) Time. A motion for new trial shall be filed not later than 10 days after return of verdict in a jury action or the date of filing of the judgment in a nonjury action. A timely motion may be amended to state new grounds at any time before it is disposed of in the discretion of the court.

(b) Determination. The motion shall set forth the basis with particularity. Upon examination of the motion, the court may find it without merit and deny it summarily, or may grant a hearing on it with notice.

(c) Grounds. All orders granting a new trial shall specify the specific grounds therefor. If such an order is appealed and does not state the specific grounds, the appellate court shall relinquish its jurisdiction to the trial court for entry of an order specifying the grounds for granting the new trial.

1972 Amendment. Subdivisions (a) and (c) are substantially the same as Florida Rule of Civil Procedure 1.530(b) and (f).

1984 Amendment. This change will be in conformity with the proposed

amendment to Florida Rule of Civil Procedure 1.530.

RULE 7.190. RELIEF FROM JUDGMENT OR ORDER; CLERICAL MISTAKES

(a) Clerical Mistakes. Clerical mistakes in judgments, orders, or other parts of the record and errors therein arising from oversight or omission may be corrected by the court at any time on its own initiative or on the motion of any party and after such notice, if any, as the court orders. During the pendency of an appeal, such mistakes may be so corrected before the record on appeal is docketed in the appellate court, and thereafter while the appeal is pending may be so corrected with leave of the appellate court.

(b) Mistakes; Inadvertence; Excusable Neglect; Newly Discovered Evidence; Fraud; etc. On motion and on such terms as are just, the court may relieve a party or a party's legal representative from a final judgment, order, or proceeding for the following reasons: (1) mistake, inadvertence, surprise, or excusable neglect; (2) newly discovered evidence which by due diligence could not have been discovered in time to move for a new trial or rehearing; (3) fraud (whether heretofore denominated intrinsic or extrinsic), misrepresentation, or other misconduct of an adverse party; (4) the judgment is void; or (5) the judgment has been satisfied, released, or discharged or a prior judgment on which it is based has been reversed or otherwise vacated or it is no longer equitable that the judgment should have prospective application. The motion shall be made within a reasonable time, and for reasons (1), (2), and (3) not more than 1 year after the judgment, order, or proceeding was entered or taken. A motion under this subdivision does not affect the finality of a judgment or suspend its operation.

RULE 7.200. EXECUTIONS

Executions on judgments shall issue during the life of the judgment on the oral request of the party entitled to it or that party's attorney without praecipe. No execution or other final process shall issue until the judgment on which it is based has been rendered or within the time for serving a motion for new trial and, if a motion for new trial is timely served, until it is determined; provided execution or other final process may be issued on special order of the court at any time after judgment.

RULE 7.210. STAY OF JUDGMENT AND EXECUTION

(a) Judgment or Execution or Levy Stayed. When judgment is to be entered against a party, the judge may inquire and permit inquiry about the earnings and financial status of the party and has discretionary power to stay an entry of judgment or, if entered, to stay execution or levy on such terms as are just and in consideration of a stipulation on the part of the judgment debtor to make such payments as will ensure a periodic reduction of the judgment until it is satisfied.

(b) Stipulation. The judge shall note the terms of such stipulation in the file; the stipulation may be set out in the judgment or made a part of the judgment by reference to "the stipulation made in open court."

(c) Execution. When judgment is entered and execution stayed pending payments, if the judgment debtor fails to pay the installment payments, the judgment creditor may have execution without further notice for the unpaid amount of the judgment upon filing an affidavit of the amount due.

(d) Oral Stipulations. Oral stipulations may be made in the presence of the court that upon failure of the judgment debtor to comply with any agreement, judgment may be entered or execution issued, or both, without further notice.

1988 Amendment. Adds the staying of levy as an alternative for the court when arranging payment. Provides lien rights priority protection for judgment creditors.

RULE 7.220. SUPPLEMENTARY PROCEEDINGS

Proceedings supplementary to execution may be had in accordance with proceedings provided by law or by the Florida Rules of Civil Procedure.

RULE 7.221. HEARING IN AID OF EXECUTION

(a) Use of Form 7.343. In any final judgment, the judge shall include the Enforcement Paragraph of form 7.340 if requested by the prevailing party or attorney. In addition to the forms of discovery available to the judgment creditor under Fla. R. Civ. P. 1.560, the judge, at the request of the judgment creditor or the judgment creditor's attorney, shall order a judgment debtor to complete form 7.343 within 30 days of the order or other such reasonable time determined by the court. If the judgment debtor fails to obey the order, Fla. R. Civ. P. Form 1.982 may be used in conjunction with this subdivision of this rule.

(b) Purpose of Hearing. The judge, at the request of the judgment creditor, shall order a judgment debtor to appear at a hearing in aid of execution at a time certain 30 or more days from the date of entry of a judgment for the purpose of inquiring of the judgment debtor under oath as to earnings, financial status, and any assets available in excess of exemptions to be applied towards satisfaction of judgment. The provisions of this subdivision of this rule shall only apply to a judgment creditor who is a natural person and was not represented by an attorney prior to judgment. Forms 7.342, 7.343, and 7.344 shall be used in connection with this subdivision of this rule.

Committee Notes

1988 Amendment. Provides a procedure for postjudgment, court-assisted discovery for natural person judgment creditors, unrepresented by counsel prior to judgment.

1996 Amendment. The purpose of the change is to make form 7.343 (Fact Information Sheet) available for use by both a party and the party's attorney, even though the hearing in aid of execution is not available to the attorney. The rule will allow the court to include the order as part of the final judgment or to issue the order after the judgment. The court may adjust the time allowed for the response to the Fact Information Sheet to fit the circumstances.

RULE 7.230. APPELLATE REVIEW

Review of orders and judgments of the courts governed by these rules shall be prosecuted in accordance with the Florida Rules of Appellate Procedure.

Committee Notes

1972 Amendment. Attention is directed to Florida Appellate Rule 4.7, which authorizes the circuit court to modify or dispense with any of the steps to be taken after filing of the notice of appeal.

Appendix C
Checklists

You can use the checklists in this appendix to be sure you do not forget any of the important parts of your case. There is one checklist for the plaintiff and one for the defendant. You may not need every step in every case.

SMALL CLAIMS CHECKLIST
FOR PLAINTIFF

❏ **Decide if you should sue.**
- ❏ Did you try to work it out with the other side?
- ❏ Is there a legal theory which would make the defendant liable?
- ❏ Do you have enough evidence to win the case?
- ❏ Does the defendant have any defenses?
- ❏ Does the defendant have any money or property you could seize?

❏ **Prepare your case.**
- ❏ Gather evidence
- ❏ Talk to witnesses
- ❏ Prepare your statement of claim
- ❏ Determine the proper venue
- ❏ File your case

❏ **Attend the pretrial conference.**
- ❏ Be prepared to explain the case clearly and quickly
- ❏ Be on time/Dress appropriately/Be polite
- ❏ Be prepared to settle if the defendant makes a good offer

❏ **Before the trial.**
- ❏ Gather all the evidence
- ❏ Subpoena witnesses and evidence if necessary

❏ **Attend the trial.**
- ❏ Be prepared
- ❏ Be on time/Dress appropriately/Be polite
- ❏ Be prepared to settle if the defendant makes a good offer

❏ **After the trial:**

If you won a countersuit—
- ❏ See if defendant plans to pay
- ❏ File judgment as a lien
- ❏ Docket judgment with sheriff
- ❏ Set hearing in aid of execution (or set deposition)
- ❏ File for garnishment

If you lost—
- ❏ Should you stipulate to avoid a judgment?
- ❏ Was it a default which can be vacated?
- ❏ Should you request a rehearing?
- ❏ Is there an issue to appeal?
- ❏ Should you pay?

SMALL CLAIMS CHECKLIST
FOR DEFENDANT

❒ **Before the pretrial conference.**
   ❒ Should you try to work it out with the other side?
   ❒ Should you file a motion for continuance?
   ❒ Should you hire a lawyer?
   ❒ Do you have a defense which would bar the claim?
   ❒ Should you countersue or file a third party complaint?

❒ **Attend the pretrial conference.**
   ❒ Be prepared to explain your side clearly and quickly
   ❒ Be on time/Dress appropriately/Be polite
   ❒ Be prepared to settle if the plaintiff makes a good offer

❒ **Before the trial.**
   ❒ Gather all the evidence
   ❒ Subpoena witnesses and evidence if necessary

❒ **Attend the trial.**
   ❒ Be prepared
   ❒ Be on time/Dress appropriately/Be polite
   ❒ Be prepared to settle if the defendant makes a good offer

❒ **After the trial:**

If you won a countersuit—
   ❒ See if plaintiff plans to pay
   ❒ File judgment as a lien
   ❒ Docket judgment with sheriff
   ❒ Set hearing in aid of execution (or set deposition)
   ❒ File for garnishment

If you lost—
   ❒ Should you stipulate to avoid a judgment?
   ❒ Was it a default which can be vacated?
   ❒ Should you request a rehearing?
   ❒ Is there an issue to appeal?
   ❒ Should you pay?

APPENDIX D

FORMS

The forms on the following pages are explained throughout the book. Some counties have their own forms and if they are available in your county you should use those. Judges and court clerks are more comfortable using forms that they have used before. But if your county does not provide forms, or if your type of claim is not covered by an available form, then use these.

COUNTY COURT,_____ COUNTY, FLORIDA
SMALL CLAIMS DIVISION
CASE NO._____

_____
_____
PLAINTIFF(S)
Address:

VS.

_____
_____
DEFENDANT(S)
Address:

STATEMENT OF CLAIM IN REPLEVIN

This is an action to recover possession of personal property in_____County, Florida, which has a value of $_____.

Plaintiff(s) is lawfully entitled to possession of the following personal property:

Plaintiff(s) source of title is_____ (a copy is attached).

The aforementioned property is wrongfully detained by the Defendant(s) having _____.

The property has not been taken for any tax, assessment or fine levied under any law of this state nor seized under any execution or attachment against the goods and chattels of Plaintiff(s) liable to execution.

Defendant(s) has possession of and detains the property at_____ _____(address).

WHEREFORE, Plaintiff(s) demand judgment for Possession of the property and damages against defendant(s) and costs.

STATE OF FLORIDA
COUNTY OF _____

Plaintiff(s)_____ state(s) that the foregoing is a just and true statement of the amount owing the Defendant(s) to the Plaintiff(s) exclusive of all set-offs and just grounds of defense. Affiant states that Defendant(s) is/are not in the military service of the United States of America.

Sworn to and subscribed before me by _____
_____ who is personally known to me

_____
Plaintiff(s) or Agent
Address:

or produced _____ as identification
this_____day of_____, _____.

_____

Telephone No._____

_____
Deputy Clerk or Notary Public
State of Florida
My commission expires:

SC 110

COUNTY COURT,_____ **COUNTY, FLORIDA**
SMALL CLAIMS DIVISION
CASE NO._____

_____
_____
PLAINTIFF(S)
Address:

VS.

_____
_____
DEFENDANT(S)
Address:

STATEMENT OF CLAIM IN REPLEVIN
Section 538.08 Florida Statutes
Plaintiff(s) sues the Defendant(s) and alleges:

1. This is an action to recover possession of personal property in_____County, Florida.

2. The description of the property is: _____
_____.
   To the best of plaintiff's knowledge, information and belief, the value of the property is $_____.

3. Plaintiff is entitled to the property under a security agreement dated _____, a copy of which is attached.

4. To plaintiff's best knowledge, information and belief, the property is located at:_____
_____.

5. The property is wrongfully detained by defendant. Defendant came into possession of the property by _____.

6. The property has not been taken under an execution or attachment against plaintiff's property.

Wherefore, plaintiff(s) demand Judgment for Possession of the property and damages against defendant(s) and costs.

STATE OF FLORIDA
COUNTY OF _____

    Plaintiff(s)_____ state(s) that the foregoing is a just and true statement of the amount owing the Defendant(s) to the Plaintiff(s) exclusive of all set-offs and just grounds of defense. Affiant states that Defendant(s) is/are not in the military service of the United States.

_____
Plaintiff(s) or Agent
Address:
_____
_____
Telephone No._____

SC 110

Sworn to and subscribed before me by _____
_____ who is personally known to me
or produced _____ as identification
this_____day of_____, _____.

_____
Deputy Clerk or Notary Public
State of Florida
My commission expires:

COUNTY COURT,_____ COUNTY, FLORIDA
SMALL CLAIMS DIVISION
CASE NO._____

_____
_____
PLAINTIFF(S)

Address:

VS.

_____
_____
DEFENDANT(S)

Address:

STATEMENT OF CLAIM IN REPLEVIN

Section 538.24 Florida Statutes

Plaintiff(s) sues the Defendant(s) and alleges:

1. This is an action to recover possession of personal property in_____County, Florida.

2. The description of the property is: _____
_____.

    To the best of plaintiff's knowledge, information and belief, the value of the property is $_____.

3. Plaintiff is the lawful owner of the property and can identify the property as belonging to the plaintiff in the following manner: _____.

4. Plaintiff is entitled to the property under a security agreement dated _____, a copy of which is attached.

4. To plaintiff's best knowledge, information and belief, the property is located at: _____
_____.

5. The property is wrongfully detained by defendant. Defendant came into possession of the property by
_____.

6. The property has not been taken under an execution or attachment against plaintiff's property.

Wherefore, plaintiff(s) demand Judgment for Possession of the property and damages against defendant(s) and costs.

STATE OF FLORIDA
COUNTY OF _____

    Plaintiff(s)_____ state(s) that the foregoing is a just and true statement of the amount owing the Defendant(s) to the Plaintiff(s) exclusive of all set-offs and just grounds of defense. Affiant states that Defendant(s) is/are not in the military service of the United States.

_____
Plaintiff(s) or Agent
Address:

_____

_____
Telephone No._____

SC 111

Sworn to and subscribed before me by _____
_____ who is personally known to me
or produced _____ as identification
this_____day of_____, _____.

_____
Deputy Clerk or Notary Public
State of Florida
My commission expires:

COUNTY COURT,_____ COUNTY, FLORIDA
SMALL CLAIMS DIVISION
CASE NO._____

_____
_____
PLAINTIFF(S)

Address:

VS.

_____
_____
DEFENDANT(S)

Address:

STATEMENT OF CLAIM—ACCOUNT—ACCOUNT STATED

Plaintiff(s) sue(s) the Defendant(s) for damages which do not exceed $5,000.00, exclusive of costs, interest and attorney's fee (if appropriate) and allege(s):

1. Before the institution of this action, Plaintiff(s) and Defendant(s) had business transactions between them, and on _____, they agreed to the resulting balance.

2. Plaintiff(s) rendered a statement of it to Defendant(s), a copy being attached, and Defendant(s) did not object to the statement.

3. Defendant(s) owe(s) Plaintiff(s) $_____ that is due with interest since _____, _____, on the account.

WHEREFORE, Plaintiff(s) demand(s) judgment in the sum of $_____ together with costs, interest and attorney's fee.

STATE OF FLORIDA
COUNTY OF _____

Plaintiff(s)_____ state(s) that the foregoing is a just and true statement of the amount owing the Defendant(s) to the Plaintiff(s) exclusive of all set-offs and just grounds of defense. Affiant states that Defendant(s) is/are not in the military service of the United States of America.

_____
Plaintiff(s) or Agent
Address:

_____

_____

Telephone No._____

SC 013

Sworn to and subscribed before me by _____
_____ who is personally known to me
or produced _____ as identification
this_____day of_____, _____.

_____
Deputy Clerk or Notary Public
State of Florida
My commission expires:

COUNTY COURT,_____ COUNTY, FLORIDA
SMALL CLAIMS DIVISION
CASE NO._____

_____
_____
PLAINTIFF(S)
Address:

VS.

_____
_____
DEFENDANT(S)
Address:

STATEMENT OF CLAIM—ACCOUNT—OPEN ACCOUNT

Plaintiff(s) sue(s) Defendant(s) for damages which do no exceed $5,000.00, exclusive of costs, interest and attorney's fee (if appropriate) and allege(s):

Defendant(s) owes Plaintiff(s) $_____ that is due with interest since _____, _____, according to the attached account.

WHEREFORE, Plaintiff(s) demand judgment in the sum of $_____ together with costs, interest and attorney's fee.

STATE OF FLORIDA
COUNTY OF_____

Plaintiff(s)_____ state(s) that the foregoing is a just and true statement of the amount owing the Defendant(s) to the Plaintiff(s) exclusive of all set-offs and just grounds of defense. Affiant states that Defendant(s) is/are not in the military service of the United States of America.

_____
Plaintiff(s) or Agent
Address:
_____

_____
Telephone No._____

Sworn to and subscribed before me by _____
_____ who is personally known to me
or produced _____ as identification
this_____day of_____, _____.

_____
Deputy Clerk or Notary Public
State of Florida
My commission expires:

SC 15

109

COUNTY COURT,_____ **COUNTY, FLORIDA**
SMALL CLAIMS DIVISION
CASE NO._____

_____

_____
PLAINTIFF(S)
Address:

VS.

_____

_____
DEFENDANT(S)
Address:

STATEMENT OF CLAIM
GOODS OR SERVICES SOLD—MONEY OWED

Plaintiff(s) sue(s) the Defendant(s) for damages which do not exceed $5,000.00, exclusive of costs, interest and attorney's fee (if appropriate) and allege(s):

1.   Defendant(s) owe(s) Plaintiff(s) $_____ that is due with interest since _____, _____, for the following (goods/services), sold and delivered/performed by Plaintiff(s) (to/for) Defendant(s) between _____, _____, and _____, _____.

_____

_____

(list the goods or services, the dates of each, and price or fee of each)

2.   The amount due and owing by Defendant(s) is $_____.

WHEREFORE, Plaintiff(s) demand judgment in the sum of $_____ together with costs, interest and attorney's fees.

STATE OF FLORIDA
COUNTY OF _____

Plaintiff(s)_____ state(s) that the foregoing is a just and true statement of the amount owing the Defendant(s) to the Plaintiff(s) exclusive of all set-offs and just grounds of defense. Affiant states that Defendant(s) is/are not in the military service of the United States of America.

_____

Plaintiff(s) or Agent
Address:

_____

Telephone No._____

SC 49

Sworn to and subscribed before me by _____ _____ who is personally known to me or produced _____ as identification this_____day of_____, _____.

_____

Deputy Clerk or Notary Public
State of Florida
My commission expires:

COUNTY COURT,_____ COUNTY, FLORIDA
SMALL CLAIMS DIVISION
CASE NO._____

_____

_____
PLAINTIFF(S)

Address:

VS.

_____

_____
DEFENDANT(S)

Address:

STATEMENT OF CLAIM

Plaintiff(s) sue(s) the Defendant(s) for damages which do not exceed $5,000.00, exclusive of costs, interest and attorney's fee (if appropriate) and allege(s):

COUNT ONE—ACCOUNT—ACCOUNT STATED

1. Before the institution of this action, Plaintiff(s) and Defendant(s) had business transactions between them, and on _____, they agreed to the resulting balance.

2. Plaintiff(s) rendered a statement of it to Defendant(s), a copy being attached, and Defendant(s) did not object to the statement.

3. Defendant(s) owe(s) Plaintiff(s) $_____ that is due with interest since _____, _____, on the account.

WHEREFORE, Plaintiff(s) demand(s) judgment in the sum of $_____ together with costs, interest and attorney's fee.

COUNT TWO—OPEN ACCOUNT

Defendant(s) owes Plaintiff(s) $_____ that is due with interest since _____, _____, according to the attached account.

WHEREFORE, Plaintiff(s) demand judgment in the sum of $_____ together with costs, interest and attorney's fee.

COUNT THREE—GOODS/SERVICES SOLD

1. Defendant(s) owe(s) Plaintiff(s) $_____ that is due with interest since _____, _____, for the following (goods/services), sold and delivered/performed by Plaintiff(s) (to/for) Defendant(s) between _____, _____, and _____, _____.

_____
(list the goods or services, the dates of each, and price or fee of each)

2. The amount due and owing by Defendant(s) is $_____.

WHEREFORE, Plaintiff(s) demand judgment in the sum of $_____ together with costs, interest and attorney's fees.

STATE OF FLORIDA

COUNTY OF _____

Plaintiff(s)_____ state(s) that the foregoing is a just and true statement of the amount owing the Defendant(s) to the Plaintiff(s) exclusive of all set-offs and just grounds of defense. Affiant states that Defendant(s) is/are not in the military service of the United States of America.

Sworn to and subscribed before me by _____

_____ who is personally known to me

_____
Plaintiff(s) or Agent
Address:

or produced _____ as identification
this_____day of_____, _____.

_____

_____

Telephone No._____

_____
Deputy Clerk or Notary Public
State of Florida
My commission expires:

111

COUNTY COURT,_____ COUNTY, FLORIDA
SMALL CLAIMS DIVISION
CASE NO._____

_____
_____
PLAINTIFF(S)
Address:

VS.

_____
_____
DEFENDANT(S)
Address:

STATEMENT OF CLAIM OF
SERVICES NOT PERFORMED OR PERFORMED IMPROPERLY

Plaintiff(s) sue(s) the Defendant(s) for damages which do not exceed $5,000.00, exclusive of costs, interest and attorney's fee (if appropriate) and allege(s):

1.   On or about _____, _____, in _____ County, Florida, Plaintiff(s) entered into an agreement with Defendant(s) to perform the following services: _____
_____
_____.

(set out what services Defendant(s) was to perform) OR (a copy of the agreement is attached)

2.   In consideration for these services, Plaintiff(s) paid the Defendant(s) $_____ on _____, _____.

3.   Defendant(s) services were not properly performed because: _____
_____. (Set out what is wrong with work)

OR

Defendant(s) performed no work after receipt of the money from Plaintiff(s).

4.   Plaintiff(s) has/have sustained damages of $_____ determined as follows:
_____
_____ (Set out exactly how the amount was determined. For instance, if another person has to re-do or complete the job, set out his bill for services or an estimate of the costs.)

WHEREFORE, Plaintiff(s) demand judgment in the sum of $_____ together with costs, interest and attorney's fee.

STATE OF FLORIDA
COUNTY OF _____

Plaintiff(s)_____ state(s) that the foregoing is a just and true statement of the amount owing the Defendant(s) to the Plaintiff(s) exclusive of all set-offs and just grounds of defense. Affiant states that Defendant(s) is/are not in the military service of the United States of America.

Sworn to and subscribed before me by _____

_____   _____ who is personally known to me
Plaintiff(s) or Agent   or produced _____ as identification
Address: this_____day of_____, _____.
_____

_____
Telephone No._____   Deputy Clerk or Notary Public
SC 19   State of Florida
                                             My commission expires:

COUNTY COURT,_____ COUNTY, FLORIDA
SMALL CLAIMS DIVISION
CASE NO._____

_____

_____
PLAINTIFF(S)
Address:

VS.

_____

_____
DEFENDANT(S)
Address:

STATEMENT OF CLAIM—PROMISSORY NOTE

Plaintiff(s) sue(s) the Defendant(s) for damages which do not exceed $5,000.00, exclusive of costs, interest and attorney's fee (if appropriate) and allege(s):

1. On _____, _____, Defendant(s) executed and delivered a promissory note, a copy of which is attached hereto.

2. The terms of payment were_____.
(Set out if not clear in note.)

3. Defendant(s) failed to pay $_____, _____
_____ (a)
the installment payment due on (date) - OR - (b) the note when due on (date) AND IF APPLICABLE "and the Plaintiff(s) elected to accelerate the payment of the balance."

4. Plaintiff(s) presently hold(s) said note.

5. Defendant(s) owe(s) Plaintiff(s) $_____ that is due with interest since _____, _____ on the note.

WHEREFORE, Plaintiff(s) demand judgment in the sum of $_____ together with costs, interest and attorney's fee.

STATE OF FLORIDA
COUNTY OF _____

Plaintiff(s)_____ state(s) that the foregoing is a just and true statement of the amount owing the Defendant(s) to the Plaintiff(s) exclusive of all set-offs and just grounds of defense. Affiant states that Defendant(s) is/are not in the military service of the United States of America.

Sworn to and subscribed before me by _____
_____ who is personally known to me

_____
Plaintiff(s) or Agent
Address:
or produced _____ as identification
this_____day of_____, _____.

_____

_____
Telephone No._____
SC25

_____
Deputy Clerk or Notary Public
State of Florida
My commission expires:

COUNTY COURT,_____ COUNTY, FLORIDA
SMALL CLAIMS DIVISION
CASE NO._____

_____
_____
PLAINTIFF(S)
Address:

VS.

_____
_____
DEFENDANT(S)
Address:

STATEMENT OF CLAIM—LANDLORD/TENANT—UNPAID RENT

Plaintiff(s) sue(s) the Defendant(s) for damages which do not exceed $5,000.00, exclusive of costs, interest and attorney's fee (if appropriate) and allege(s):

1. On or about _____, _____, Plaintiff(s), Landlord(s), leased to Defendant(s), Tenant(s), premises located at_____ County, Florida.

2. The lease was an oral lease containing the following provisions:_____

_____, _____.
(length of lease in months or years; amount of rent payment, notice requirement for vacating the premises; amount of security deposit, and amount of prepaid last month's rent, if any) - OR - "A copy of written lease attached."

3. Defendant(s) vacated the premises on or about _____, _____.

4. Defendant(s) failed to pay rent for the periods of _____, leaving rent due and owing of $_____.

WHEREFORE Plaintiff(s) demand judgment in the sum of $_____ together with costs, interest, and attorney's fee.

STATE OF FLORIDA
COUNTY OF _____

Plaintiff(s)_____ state(s) that the foregoing is a just and true statement of the amount owing the Defendant(s) to the Plaintiff(s) exclusive of all set-offs and just grounds of defense. Affiant states that Defendant(s) is/are not in the military service of the United States of America.

_____
Plaintiff(s) or Agent
Address:
_____
_____
Telephone No._____

SC44

Sworn to and subscribed before me by _____
_____ who is personally known to me
or produced _____ as identification
this_____day of_____, _____.

_____
Deputy Clerk or Notary Public
State of Florida
My commission expires:

COUNTY COURT,_____ COUNTY, FLORIDA
SMALL CLAIMS DIVISION
CASE NO._____

_____
_____
PLAINTIFF(S)
Address:

VS.

_____
_____
DEFENDANT(S)
Address:

STATEMENT OF CLAIM

LANDLORD/TENANT—DAMAGES TO PREMISES AND UNPAID RENT

Plaintiff(s) sue(s) the Defendant(s) for damages which do not exceed $5,000.00, exclusive of costs, interest and attorney's fee (if appropriate) and allege(s):

COUNT I

1. On or about _____, _____, Plaintiff(s), Landlord(s), leased to Defendant(s), Tenant(s), premises located at _____,
_____County, Florida.

2. The lease was an oral lease containing the following provisions: _____
_____ (Set out length of lease in months or years; amount of rent payment, the notice requirement for vacating the premises; amount of security deposit; and, the amount of prepaid last month's rent, if any.) - OR - "A copy of the written lease is attached."

3. Defendant(s) vacated premises on or about _____, _____.

4. Defendant(s) left damages in the amount of $_____, as follows:

(item)	$_____ (amount)	(item)	$_____ (amount)
(item)	$_____ (amount)	(item)	$_____ (amount)

(Attach separate sheet if necessary)

WHEREFORE, Plaintiff(s) demand judgment in the sum of $_____, together with costs, interest and attorney's fee.

COUNT II

1. On or about _____, _____, Plaintiff(s), Landlord(s), leased to Defendant(s), Tenant(s), premises located at _____, _____ County, Florida.

2. The lease was an oral lease containing the provisions as set out in paragraph 2. of Count I of this statement of Claim. - OR - A copy of the written lease is attached.

3. Defendant(s) failed to pay rent for the period of _____, _____, leaving rent due and owing of $_____.

4. Defendant(s) vacated the premises on or about _____, _____.

WHEREFORE, Plaintiff(s) demand judgment in the sum of $_____, together with costs, interest and attorney's fee.

STATE OF FLORIDA
COUNTY OF

Plaintiff(s)_____ state(s) that the foregoing is a just and true statement of the amount owing the Defendant(s) to the Plaintiff(s) exclusive of all set-offs and just grounds of defense. Affiant states that Defendant(s) is/are not in the military service of the United States of America.

Sworn to and subscribed before me by _____

_____ who is personally known to me

_____
Plaintiff(s) or Agent
Address:

or produced _____ as identification

this_____day of_____, _____.

_____

_____

Telephone No._____

SC 57

Deputy Clerk or Notary Public
State of Florida
My commission expires:

COUNTY COURT,_____ COUNTY, FLORIDA
SMALL CLAIMS DIVISION
CASE NO._____

_____
_____
PLAINTIFF(S)

Address:

VS.

_____
_____
DEFENDANT(S)

Address:

STATEMENT OF CLAIM—LANDLORD/TENANT—SECURITY DEPOSIT REFUND

    Plaintiff(s) sue(s) the Defendant(s) for damages which do not exceed $5,000.00, exclusive of costs, interest and attorney's fee (if appropriate) and allege(s):

    1. On or about _____, _____, Plaintiff(s) leased _____ (an apartment/ residence) located at _____, _____County, Florida, from Defendant(s).

    2. The lease was an oral lease containing the following provisions: _____
_____
_____

(Length of lease in months or years; amount of rent payment, notice requirement for vacating the premises; amount of security deposit, and amount of prepaid last month's rent, if any) - OR - "A copy of written lease attached."

    3. Plaintiff(s) vacated the premises on or about _____, _____.

    4. Plaintiff(s) demanded return of (**security deposit** or **last month's rent**) by _____
_____

(in person request to - name and title of person - on whatever date; or by certified letter mailed to - name and title of person - on whatever date; or set out by whatever method used).

    5. Defendant(s) has/have refused to return the **security deposit** or **last month's rent** requested.

    WHEREFORE, Plaintiff(s) demand judgment in the sum of $_____ together with costs, interest and attorney's fees.

STATE OF FLORIDA
COUNTY OF _____

    Plaintiff(s)_____ state(s) that the foregoing is a just and true statement of the amount owing the Defendant(s) to the Plaintiff(s) exclusive of all set-offs and just grounds of defense. Affiant states that Defendant(s) is/are not in the military service of the United States of America.

_____
Plaintiff(s) or Agent
Address:
_____
_____
Telephone No._____

Sworn to and subscribed before me by _____
_____ who is personally known to me
or produced _____ as identification
this_____day of_____, _____.

_____
Deputy Clerk or Notary Public
State of Florida
My commission expires:

SC 46

116

COUNTY COURT,_____ COUNTY, FLORIDA
SMALL CLAIMS DIVISION
CASE NO._____

_____
_____
PLAINTIFF(S)
Address:

VS.

_____
_____
DEFENDANT(S)
Address:

STATEMENT OF CLAIM—BAD CHECK

Plaintiff(s) sue(s) the Defendant(s) for damages which do not exceed $5,000.00, exclusive of costs, interest and attorney's fee (if appropriate) and allege(s):

1. On _____, _____, Plaintiff(s) received a bank check from Defendant(s) delivered _____ (personally by Defendant(s), or by mail, or state by what means) drawn on the _____ _____(name and address of bank check was drawn on) dated _____, _____ (date check was written).

2. The check was given to Plaintiff(s) for _____
(state whatever reason).

3. Plaintiff(s) presented this check to the above bank, and payment was refused and the checked marked (Insufficient Funds, Account Closed).

IF APPROPRIATE ADD:

4. Plaintiff(s) has/have contacted the Defendant(s) by (telephone, letter or state whatever other means contact was made)

_____ and the Defendant(s) refused to pay the amount of the check.

WHEREFORE, Plaintiff(s) demand judgment pursuant to §68.065 F.S. in the amount of $_____ together with a service charge of $_____ together with costs, interest and attorney's fees.

STATE OF FLORIDA
COUNTY OF

Plaintiff(s)_____ state(s) that the foregoing is a just and true statement of the amount owing the Defendant(s) to the Plaintiff(s) exclusive of all set-offs and just grounds of defense. Affiant states that Defendant(s) is/are not in the military service of the United States of America.

_____
Plaintiff(s) or Agent
Address:
_____
_____
Telephone No._____

Sworn to and subscribed before me by _____
_____ who is personally known to me
or produced _____ as identification
this_____day of_____, _____.

_____
Deputy Clerk or Notary Public
State of Florida
My commission expires:

SC 53

COUNTY COURT,_____ COUNTY, FLORIDA
SMALL CLAIMS DIVISION
CASE NO._____

_____
_____
PLAINTIFF(S)

Address:

VS.

_____
_____
DEFENDANT(S)

Address:

STATEMENT OF CLAIM—BAD CHECK—TRIPLE DAMAGES

Plaintiff(s) sue(s) the Defendant(s) for damages which do not exceed $5,000.00, exclusive of costs, interest and attorney's fee (if appropriate) and allege(s):

1. On _____, _____, Plaintiff(s) received a bank check from Defendant(s) delivered _____ (personally by Defendant(s), or by mail, or state by what means) drawn on the _____ _____(name and address of bank check was drawn on) dated _____, _____ (date check was written).

2. The check was given to Plaintiff(s) for _____
(state whatever reason).

3. Plaintiff(s) presented this check to the above bank, and payment was refused and the checked marked (Insufficient Funds, Account Closed).

IF APPROPRIATE ADD:

4. Plaintiff(s) has/have sent Defendant(s) notice under Florida statutes §68.065 (a copy of which is attached) and Defendant(s) has/have failed to pay said check.

_____ and the Defendant(s) refused to pay the amount of the check.

WHEREFORE, Plaintiff(s) demand judgment pursuant to Section 68.065 F.S. in the triple sum of $_____ plus service charge of $_____, (service charge of $25 if face value does not exceed $300, service charge of $40 if face value exceeds $300, or 5% of the face amount of the check, whichever is greater), costs, interest and attorney fee.

STATE OF FLORIDA
COUNTY OF

Plaintiff(s)_____ state(s) that the foregoing is a just and true statement of the amount owing the Defendant(s) to the Plaintiff(s) exclusive of all set-offs and just grounds of defense. Affiant states that Defendant(s) is/are not in the military service of the United States of America.

_____
Plaintiff(s) or Agent
Address:

_____

_____

Telephone No._____

SC 53

Sworn to and subscribed before me by _____
_____ who is personally known to me
or produced _____ as identification
this_____day of_____, _____.

_____
Deputy Clerk or Notary Public
State of Florida
My commission expires:

118

NOTICE

To: _____

_____

_____

Re: Your Check No._____

Criminal remedies:

Pursuant to Florida Statutes, section 832.07:

You are hereby notified that a check numbered_____ in the face amount of $_____, issued by you on_____, _____ drawn upon _____(bank) and payable to _____ has been dishonored. Pursuant to Florida law, you have 7 days from receipt of this notice to tender payment in cash of the full amount of the check plus a service charge of $25, if the face value does exceeds $50 but does not exceed $300, $40, if the face value exceeds $300, or 5 percent of the face amount of the check, whichever is greater, the total being $_____ and _____ cents. Unless this amount is paid in full within the time specified above, the holder of such check may turn over the dishonored check and all other available information relating to this incident to the state attorney for criminal prosecution. You may be additionally liable in a civil action for triple the amount of the check, but in no case less than $50, together with the amount of the check, a service charge, court costs, reasonable attorney fees and incurred bank fees, as provided in section 68.065.

Civil remedies:

Pursuant to Florida Statutes, section 68.065:

You are hereby notified that a check numbered_____ in the face amount of $_____, issued by you on_____, _____ drawn upon _____(bank) and payable to _____ has been dishonored. Pursuant to Florida law, you have 30 days from receipt of this notice to tender payment in cash of the full amount of the check plus a service charge of $25, if the face value does exceeds $50 but does not exceed $300, $40, if the face value exceeds $300, or 5 percent of the face amount of the check, whichever is greater, the total being $_____ and _____ cents. Unless this amount is paid in full within the 30-day period, the holder of the check or instrument may file a civil action against you for three times the amount of the check, but in no case less than $50, in addition to the payment of the check plus any court costs, reasonable attorney fees, and any bank fees incurred by the payee taking this action.

Payment should be made to: _____

_____

_____

Sent by Certified Mail, return receipt requested.

COUNTY COURT,_____ COUNTY, FLORIDA
SMALL CLAIMS DIVISION
CASE NO._____

_____
_____
PLAINTIFF(S)

Address:

VS.

_____
_____
DEFENDANT(S)

Address:

STATEMENT OF CLAIM—BREACH OF CONTRACT

Plaintiff(s) sue(s) the Defendant(s) for damages which do not exceed $5,000.00, exclusive of costs, interest and attorney's fee (if appropriate) and allege(s):

1. On _____, _____, Plaintiff(s) and Defendant(s) entered into a(n) oral/written contract.

2. The terms of the contract provided for the following: _____ _____ (set out terms) - OR - "A copy of the written contract is attached."

3. The Defendant(s) failed to fulfill the terms of the contract because the Defendant(s) _____ _____ (set out breach of contract).

4. Plaintiff(s) is/are suing for $_____ because of the breach of contract, which amount Plaintiff(s) determined as follows: _____ _____.

WHEREFORE, Plaintiff(s) demand judgment in the sum of $_____ together with costs, interest and attorney's fee.

STATE OF FLORIDA
COUNTY OF _____

Plaintiff(s)_____ state(s) that the foregoing is a just and true statement of the amount owing the Defendant(s) to the Plaintiff(s) exclusive of all set-offs and just grounds of defense. Affiant states that Defendant(s) is/are not in the military service of the United States of America.

_____
Plaintiff(s) or Agent
Address:

_____

Telephone No._____

Sworn to and subscribed before me by _____
_____ who is personally known to me
or produced _____ as identification
this_____day of_____, _____.

_____
Deputy Clerk or Notary Public
State of Florida
My commission expires:

COUNTY COURT,_____ COUNTY, FLORIDA
SMALL CLAIMS DIVISION
CASE NO._____

_____
_____
PLAINTIFF(S)

Address:

VS.

_____
_____
DEFENDANT(S)

Address:

STATEMENT OF CLAIM—AUTO ACCIDENT

Plaintiff(s) sue(s) the Defendant(s) for damages which do not exceed $5,000.00, exclusive of costs, interest and attorney's fee (if appropriate) and allege(s):

1. On _____, _____, Defendant(s) owned and/or operated a motor vehicle at _____ (place), _____, County, Florida.

2. At the time, the Defendant(s) negligently operated or maintained the motor vehicle so that a collision occurred between Plaintiff(s) _____ (motor vehicle or property) and Defendant(s) motor vehicle.

3. As a result, Plaintiff(s) was/were injured and/or sustained damages to his/her motor vehicle or property.

4. Plaintiff(s) motor vehicle or property is _____
_____ (description of automobile or property).

WHEREFORE, Plaintiff(s) demand judgment in the sum of $_____ determined as follows: _____ together with costs, interest and attorney's fee.
STATE OF FLORIDA
COUNTY OF _____

Plaintiff(s)_____ state(s) that the foregoing is a just and true statement of the amount owing the Defendant(s) to the Plaintiff(s) exclusive of all set-offs and just grounds of defense. Affiant states that Defendant(s) is/are not in the military service of the United States of America.

_____
Plaintiff(s) or Agent
Address:

_____

_____
Telephone No._____

Sworn to and subscribed before me by _____
_____ who is personally known to me
or produced _____ as identification
this_____day of_____, _____.

_____
Deputy Clerk or Notary Public
State of Florida
My commission expires:

SC 56

COUNTY COURT,_____ COUNTY, FLORIDA
SMALL CLAIMS DIVISION
CASE NO._____

_____
_____
PLAINTIFF(S)
Address:

VS.

_____
_____
DEFENDANT(S)
Address:

NOTICE OF FILING OF FOREIGN JUDGMENT

The Clerk of the Circuit/County Court of _____ County, Florida, hereby gives notice that pursuant to Section **55.501-509**, Florida Statutes, quoted below, a judgment rendered against you in the State of _____ on _____ , _____, was filed with the Clerk on _____, _____, and has been recorded in the Official Records of _____ County, Florida at O.R. Book _____, page _____. Copies of said judgment and the supporting affidavit filed therewith are attached to this Notice.

The aforesaid law provides:

Section 55.503, Recording and status of foreign judgments; fees——
A copy of any foreign judgment certified in accordance with the laws of the United States or of this state may be recorded in the office of the Clerk of the Circuit Court of any county. The Clerk shall file, record and index the foreign judgment in the same manner as a judgment of a circuit or county court of this state. A judgment so recorded shall have the same effect and shall be subject to the same rules of civil procedure, legal and equitable defenses, and proceedings for reopening, vacating, or staying judgments and may be enforced, released or satisfied as a judgment of a circuit or county court of this state.

Section 55.505, Notice of Recording; prerequisite to enforcement --Subsection (3),
No execution of other process for enforcement of a foreign judgment recorded hereunder shall issue until 30 days after the mailing of notice by the clerk. When an action authorized in subsection §55.509(1) is filed it shall act as an automatic stay of the effect of this section.

Section 55.507, Lien; when effective --
A foreign judgment shall not operate as a lien until 30 days after the mailing of the notice by the Clerk. When an action authorized in §55.509(1) is filed, it shall act as an automatic stay of the effect of this section.

Section 55.509, Stay of enforcement of judgment --
Subsection (1) If, within 30 days after the date the foreign judgment is recorded, the judgment debtor files an action contesting the jurisdiction of the court which entered the foreign judgment or the validity of the foreign judgment and records a lis pendens directed toward the foreign judgment the court shall stay enforcement of the foreign judgment and the judgment lien upon the filing of the action by the judgment debtor.

Subsection (2) If the judgment debtor shows the circuit or county court any ground upon which enforcement of a judgment of any circuit or county court of this state would be stayed, the court shall stay enforcement of the foreign judgment for an appropriate period, upon requiring the same security for satisfaction of the judgment which is required in this state.

The name and post office address of the judgment creditor (or his Florida attorney) are as follows:

_____
_____
_____

Any pleadings filed with the Clerk regarding this matter should include the Small Claims Case Number assigned above.

DATED and mailed this _____ day of _____, _____.

CLERK OF THE COUNTY COURT

BY:_____
Deputy Clerk

COUNTY COURT,_____ COUNTY, FLORIDA
SMALL CLAIMS DIVISION
CASE NO._____

_____
_____
PLAINTIFF(S)
Address:

VS.

_____
_____
DEFENDANT(S)
Address:

STATEMENT OF CLAIM—EXPRESS WARRANTY

Plaintiff(s) sue(s) the Defendant(s) for damages which do not exceed $5,000.00, exclusive of costs, interest and attorney's fee (if appropriate) and allege(s):

1. On or about _____, _____, Plaintiff(s) and Defendant(s) had certain business transactions in which Plaintiff(s) agreed to pay the Defendant(s) $_____ for which Defendant(s) would _____

_____

(Insert what the Defendant was to do, i.e., sell something to Plaintiff, repair something or perform some other service, set out specifically.)

2. Plaintiff(s) paid said amount to Defendant(s).

3. At the time of the above-described _____ (sale, service, or repair) Defendant(s) _____ (delivered to Plaintiff a written warranty, a copy of which is attached as Exhibit "A" OR orally represented to the Plaintiff that — insert precisely as possible what part, product or service he agreed to perform for the Plaintiff, if trouble occurred.)

4. Plaintiff(s) relied on said express warranty when entering into the subject transaction and was/were induced into the transaction by said warranty.

5. Defendant(s) failed to abide by said express warranty on _____, _____, by _____ (set out the action or nonaction which is alleged to breach the warranty described in paragraph 3.)

6. As a result of said breach, Plaintiff(s) has/have been damaged in the amount of $_____, determined by Plaintiff(s) as follows: _____ (Set out how damages determined.)

WHEREFORE, Plaintiff(s) demand judgment in the sum of $_____ together with costs, interest and attorney's fees.

STATE OF FLORIDA
COUNTY OF _____

Plaintiff(s)_____ state(s) that the foregoing is a just and true statement of the amount owing the Defendant(s) to the Plaintiff(s) exclusive of all set-offs and just grounds of defense. Affiant states that Defendant(s) is/are not in the military service of the United States of America.

_____
Plaintiff(s) or Agent
Address:
_____
_____
Telephone No._____

Sworn to and subscribed before me by _____ _____ who is personally known to me or produced _____ as identification this_____day of_____, _____.

_____
Deputy Clerk or Notary Public
State of Florida
My commission expires:

SC 17B

123

COUNTY COURT,_____ COUNTY, FLORIDA
SMALL CLAIMS DIVISION
CASE NO._____

_____
_____
PLAINTIFF(S)

Address:

VS.

_____
_____
DEFENDANT(S)

Address:

STATEMENT OF CLAIM

Plaintiff(s) sue(s) the Defendant(s) for damages which do not exceed $5,000.00, exclusive of costs, interest and attorney's fee for (as checked (X) below):

( )   Goods, wares and merchandise sold by Plaintiff(s) to Defendant(s).

( )   Work done and materials furnished by Plaintiff(s) to Defendant(s).

( )   Money loaned by Plaintiff(s) to Defendant(s).

( )   On a written instrument, copy of which is attached hereto.

( )   (Rent) (Security Deposit) for certain premises in _____,County, Florida located at _____.

( )   Other (explain)

( )   Any additional facts in connection with any of the above: (Use additional sheets if necessary).

_____
_____
_____
_____

WHEREFORE, Plaintiff(s) demand judgment in the sum of $_____ together with costs, interest and attorney's fees.

STATE OF FLORIDA
COUNTY OF

Plaintiff(s)_____ state(s) that the foregoing is a just and true statement of the amount owing the Defendant(s) to the Plaintiff(s) exclusive of all set-offs and just grounds of defense. Affiant states that Defendant(s) is/are not in the military service of the United States of America.

_____
Plaintiff(s) or Agent
Address:

_____

_____

Telephone No._____

Sworn to and subscribed before me by _____
_____ who is personally known to me
or produced _____ as identification
this_____day of_____, _____.

_____
Deputy Clerk or Notary Public
State of Florida
My commission expires:

SC 2

124

COUNTY COURT,_____ **COUNTY, FLORIDA**
SMALL CLAIMS DIVISION
CASE NO._____

_____
_____
PLAINTIFF(S)
Address:

VS.

_____
_____
DEFENDANT(S)
Address:

MOTION FOR SPECIAL PROCESS SERVER

Plaintiff(s) move(s) this Honorable Court to authorize Special Process Server _____, who is not a party to this action, who is competent and over the age of 21 years, and who has no interest in and will not benefit from this action, pursuant to Florida Statutes 58.021(3) and Rules of Civil Procedure, 1.070(b) to serve the summons and complaint on _____.

DATED this _____ day of _____, _____.

_____
Plaintiff(s)

Address:

Telephone:

ORDER

THIS CAUSE having come on to be heard on Plaintiff's Motion for Special Process Server, and after being duly advised in the premises, it is

ORDERED & ADJUDGED that _____ who is not a party to this action, who is competent and over the age of 21 years, and who has no interest in and will not benefit from this action, pursuant to Florida Statute 58.021(3) and Rules of Civil Procedure, 1.070(b) is hereby authorized to serve the Summons and Complaint in the above cause on _____.

DONE AND ORDERED in Chambers in _____,

_____ County, Florida, this _____ day of _____,_____.

SC21

_____
Judge

125

COUNTY COURT,_____ COUNTY, FLORIDA
SMALL CLAIMS DIVISION
CASE NO._____

_____
_____
PLAINTIFF(S)
Address:

VS.

_____
_____
DEFENDANT(S)
Address:

AFFIDAVIT OF INABILITY TO PAY COSTS

Affiant being first duly sworn on oath deposes and says that he/she is unable to pay the charges, costs or fees in this cause either in whole or in part; that he/she has no property or other means of payment either in his/her possession or under his/her control and that he/she has not divested himself/herself of any property, either real or personal, for the purpose of receiving benefit from his/her oath; that he/she, at this time, is without funds to pay costs and unless this Court takes and enters an Order waiving costs, he/she will be deprived of his/her rights under the law in such cases made and provided. This affiant offers himself/herself up to the Court for the purpose of further examination into his/her inability to pay costs.

_____
Plaintiff(s)

Sworn to and subscribed before me this _____ day of _____, _____

_____
Deputy Clerk   Notary

ORDER OF WAIVER OF COSTS

The above named Plaintiff, being before the Court and the said Plaintiff having filed in this Court his Affidavit of Inability to Pay Costs; and testimony having been taken before the court; and the court being otherwise fully advised in the premises, it is, thereupon

ORDERED AND ADJUDGED that the Plaintiff be, and he is hereby, declared to be unable to pay costs within the meaning of section 34.041, Florida Statutes.

DONE AND ORDERED this _____ day of _____, _____.

SC94

_____
County Judge

COUNTY COURT,_____ **COUNTY, FLORIDA**
SMALL CLAIMS DIVISION
CASE NO._____

_____
_____
PLAINTIFF(S)

Address:

VS.

_____
_____
DEFENDANT(S)

Address:

REQUEST FOR ALIAS OR PLURIES SERVICE

COMES NOW the Plaintiff(s), _____,
and respectfully requests the Clerk issue a summons in the above styled cause to issue:

☐ ALIAS NOTICE TO APPEAR ☐ PLURIES NOTICE TO APPEAR

in the above styled cause to:

_____

_____

to be served by: ☐SHERIFF ☐CERTIFIED MAIL ☐PROCESS SERVER

IT IS FURTHER requested this cause be re-set for Pretrial Conference.

_____
Plaintiff

_____
Address

_____

SC87

_____
Date

COUNTY COURT,_____ COUNTY, FLORIDA
SMALL CLAIMS DIVISION
CASE NO._____

_____
_____
PLAINTIFF(S)

Address:

VS.

_____
_____
DEFENDANT(S)

Address:

THIRD PARTY COMPLAINT

Defendant/Third Party Plaintiff sues the Third Party Defendant for damages which do not exceed $5,000 exclusive of costs, interest and attorney's fee for (as checked (X) below):

( ) Goods, wares and merchandise sold by Plaintiff(s) to Defendant(s).
( ) Work done and materials furnished by Plaintiff(s) to Defendant(s).
( ) Money loaned by Plaintiff(s) to Defendant(s).
( ) On a written instrument, copy of which is attached hereto.
( ) (Rent) (Security Deposit) for certain premises in _____,County, Florida
     located at _____.
( ) Other (explain) _____.
( ) Any additional facts in connection with any of the above: (Use additional sheets if necessary).

_____
_____

WHEREFORE, Defendant/Third Party Plaintiff demands judgment in the sum of $_____ together with costs, interest and attorney's fee.

STATE OF FLORIDA
COUNTY OF _____

Defendant/Third Party Plaintiff(s) _____, states that the foregoing is a just and true statement of the amount owing by Third Party Defendant(s) to the Defendant/Third Party Plaintiff exclusive of all set-offs and just grounds of defense. Affiant states that Defendant(s) is/are not in the military service of the United States of America.

_____
Plaintiff(s) or Agent
Address:

_____

_____
Telephone No._____

Sworn to and subscribed before me by _____
_____ who is personally known to me
or produced _____ as identification
this_____day of_____, _____.

_____
Deputy Clerk or Notary Public
State of Florida
My commission expires:

SC 75

128

COUNTY COURT,_____ COUNTY, FLORIDA
SMALL CLAIMS DIVISION
CASE NO._____

_____
_____
PLAINTIFF(S)/COUNTER DEFENDANT(S)
Address:

VS.

_____
_____
DEFENDANT(S)/COUNTER PLAINTIFF(S)
Address:

STATEMENT OF COUNTERCLAIM

Defendant(s)/Counter-Plaintiff(s) sue(s) the Plaintiff(s)/Counter-Defendant(s) for damages which do not exceed $5,000 exclusive of costs, interest and attorney's fee for (as checked (X) below):

( ) Goods, wares and merchandise sold by Plaintiff(s) to Defendant(s).
( ) Work done and materials furnished by Plaintiff(s) to Defendant(s).
( ) Money loaned by Plaintiff(s) to Defendant(s).
( ) On a written instrument, copy of which is attached hereto.
( ) (Rent) (Security Deposit) for certain premises in _____,County, Florida located at _____.
( ) Other (explain) _____.
( ) Any additional facts in connection with any of the above: (Use additional sheets if necessary).

_____
_____

WHEREFORE, Defendant(s)/Counter-Plaintiff(s) demand judgment in the sum of $_____ together with costs, interest and attorney's fee.

STATE OF FLORIDA
COUNTY OF _____

Defendant(s)/Counter-Plaintiff(s) _____, states that the foregoing is a just and true statement of the amount owing by Plaintiff(s)/Counter-Defendant(s) to the Defendant(s)/Counter-Plaintiff(s) exclusive of all set-offs and just grounds of defense. Affiant states that Defendant(s) is/are not in the military service of the United States of America.

_____
Plaintiff(s) or Agent
Address:

_____

_____
Telephone No._____

SC 76

Sworn to and subscribed before me by _____
_____ who is personally known to me
or produced _____ as identification
this_____day of_____, _____.

_____
Deputy Clerk or Notary Public
State of Florida
My commission expires:

129

form 24

COUNTY COURT,_____ **COUNTY, FLORIDA**
SMALL CLAIMS DIVISION
CASE NO._____

_____
_____
                    Plaintiff(s)

Address:

VS.

_____
_____
        Defendant(s)/Cross Claim Plaintiff(s)

_____
_____
Defendant(s)/Cross Claim Defendant(s)
Address:

STATEMENT OF CROSS-CLAIM

    Defendant(s)/Cross-Claimant Plaintiff(s) sues the Defendant/Cross-Claimant Defendant for damages which do not exceed $5,000 exclusive of costs, interest and attorney's fee for (as checked (X) below):

( )   Goods, wares and merchandise sold by Plaintiff(s) to Defendant(s).
( )   Work done and materials furnished by Plaintiff(s) to Defendant(s).
( )   Money loaned by Plaintiff(s) to Defendant(s).
( )   On a written instrument, copy of which is attached hereto.
( )   (Rent) (Security Deposit) for certain premises in _____,
    County, Florida located at _____.
( )   Other (explain)
( )   Any additional facts in connection with any of the above: (Use additional sheets if necessary).

_____
_____

WHEREFORE, Defendant/Cross-Claimant Plaintiff demands judgment in the sum of $_____ together with costs, interest and attorney's fee.

STATE OF FLORIDA
COUNTY OF _____

    Defendant/Cross-Claimant Plaintiff(s) states that the foregoing is a just and true statement of the amount owing by Defendant/Cross-Claimant Defendant(s) to Defendant/ Cross-Claimant Plaintiff(s) exclusive of all set-offs and just grounds of defense. Affiant states that Defendant(s) is/are not in the military service of the United States of America.

    Defendant/Cross-Claimant Plaintiff further certifies that this action is brought in the county in which venue is proper, pursuant to Rules of Summary Procedure and Florida Statutes.

_____
Plaintiff(s) or Agent
Address:

_____

_____

Telephone No._____

SC 77

Sworn to and subscribed before me by _____
_____ who is personally known to me
or produced _____ as identification
this_____day of_____, _____.

_____
Deputy Clerk or Notary Public
State of Florida
My commission expires:

130

COUNTY COURT,_____ COUNTY, FLORIDA
SMALL CLAIMS DIVISION
CASE NO._____

_____
_____
PLAINTIFF(S)

Address:

VS.

_____
_____
DEFENDANT(S)

Address:

PRAECIPE FOR SUBPOENA

COMES NOW the Plaintiff/Defendant, _____

_____

and respectfully requests the Clerk to issue:
- ☐ SUBPOENA DUCES TECUM
- ☐ WITNESS SUBPOENA FOR TRIAL
- ☐ SUBPOENA FOR TRIAL
- ☐ WITNESS SUBPOENA VIA TELEPHONE CONFERENCE CALL

in the above-styled case to:

_____

_____

and further,

☐ TO PRODUCE ON _____ at _____o'clock at:

_____

the following:
1. _____
2. _____
3. _____
4. _____

☐ TO APPEAR: ☐ FOR TRIAL   ☐ VIA TELEPHONE CONFERENCE CALL ON
_____ at _____ o'clock before the Honorable
_____ at

_____

_____
Plaintiff/Defendant

SC 86

_____
_____
Address
Phone: _____
Date: _____

COUNTY COURT,_____ COUNTY, FLORIDA
SMALL CLAIMS DIVISION
CASE NO._____

_____
_____
PLAINTIFF(S)

Address:

VS.

_____
_____
DEFENDANT(S)

Address:

SUBPOENA

THE STATE OF FLORIDA
TO:

     YOU ARE HEREBY COMMANDED to appear before the Honorable _____
_____, one of the Judges of our said Court, at _____,
Florida, on _____, _____, at _____M., to testify in the above styled
cause. If you fail to appear, you may be in contempt of Court.

     You are subpoenaed to appear by _____and
unless excused from this subpoena by _____ or the Court, you
shall respond to this subpoena as directed.

     WITNESS, _____, as Clerk of the County Court, and the seal
of said Court, at the Courthouse at _____, Florida.

_____
Date

(SEAL)

_____
CLERK OF THE COUNTY COURT

BY:_____
Deputy Clerk

_____
Plaintiff/Defendant
Address:

SC 22

form 27

COUNTY COURT,_____ COUNTY, FLORIDA
SMALL CLAIMS DIVISION
CASE NO._____

_____
_____
PLAINTIFF(S)
Address:

VS.

_____
_____
DEFENDANT(S)
Address:

SUBPOENA DUCES TECUM

THE STATE OF FLORIDA
TO:

YOU ARE HEREBY COMMANDED to appear before the Honorable _____, one of the Judges of our said Court, at _____ County Courthouse at _____, Florida, on _____, _____, at _____M., to testify in the above styled cause and to have with you at said time and place the following:

If you fail to appear, you may be in contempt of court.

You are subpoenaed to appear by _____ and unless excused from this subpoena by _____ or the Court, you shall respond to this subpoena as directed.

WITNESS my hand and seal of said Court on _____, _____.

_____
CLERK OF COUNTY COURT

(SEAL)

BY:_____
Deputy Clerk

SC 21

IN THE COUNTY COURT, IN AND FOR _____
COUNTY, FLORIDA SMALL CLAIM COURT
CASE NO._____

_____   _____

_____   _____
Plaintiff(s)   Address

vs.

_____   _____

_____   _____
Defendant(s)   Address

STIPULATION TO STAY ENTRY OF JUDGMENT

The Plaintiff(s) _____ and the
Defendant(s)   _____ stipulate
as follows:

1. The Defendant(s) agree(s) to pay and the Plaintiff(s) agree(s) to accept:
   A. Principle amount $_____
   B. Plus interest of $_____ to date(plus an additional interest charge
      of_____% per annum on the unpaid balance)
   C. Plus Attorney's fee of $_____
   D. Plus Court costs in the amount of $_____
   E. The above makes a total sum of $_____ to be paid in payments of
      $_____ beginning _____, until the total indebtedness is paid in full.
2. The Defendant(s) and Plaintiff(s) agree that upon the Defendant's default of the terms of this Stipulation, a
   Final Judgment will be entered in favor of the Plaintiff(s) in the amount of $_____ (minus
   payments made) upon the filing of a sworn statement with the Court reciting the balance claimed due.
3. Upon Defendant's completion of payment according to the terms of the Stipulation, Plaintiff(s) agree to voluntarily dismiss this action with prejudice by notice to the Clerk, <u>in writing</u>, that the claim has been fully satisfied.

DATED this _____ day of _____, _____.

_____   _____

_____   _____
Plaintiff(s)   Defendant(s)

ORDER

UPON CONSIDERATION of the Stipulation between the parties in this cause, it is ORDERED and
ADJUDGED as follows:
1. That entry of Final Judgment is stayed pending compliance with the above Stipulation which is herewith
   approved. No execution or other final process shall issue and recordation in Judgment lien record is stayed
   pending payment by the Defendant(s).
2. That upon notice to the Court of Defendant(s) default pursuant to Paragraph 2 of the above Stipulation, a
   Final Judgment will be entered.
3. That upon written notification by Plaintiff(s) that the Stipulation has been fully satisfied, the case shall be
   dismissed without further Order of the Court.
ORDERED in_____ , Pinellas County, Florida, this _____ day of _____, _____

_____
COUNTY COURT JUDGE

Copies furnished to:

COUNTY COURT,_____ **COUNTY, FLORIDA**
SMALL CLAIMS DIVISION
CASE NO._____

_____
_____
PLAINTIFF(S)
Address:

VS.

_____
_____
DEFENDANT(S)
Address:

AFFIDAVIT
(Balance Due on Stipulation)

STATE OF FLORIDA   :
COUNTY OF _____ : ss.

    Before me, the undersigned personally appeared _____,
who, by me first duly sworn, states:

    1. That he/she is the Plaintiff(s) who entered into the written stipulation filed in this cause.

    2. That the Defendant(s) _____ has failed to make payment(s) pursuant to that agreement.

    3. The last payment was made on _____, _____.

    4. The balance left due and owing under the agreement is principal and $_____costs.

    WHEREFORE, Plaintiff(s) request the court to enter a Judgement for $ _____.

_____
Plaintiff(s)

SWORN TO AND SUBSCRIBED before me at _____,
this _____ day of _____, _____.

_____
Deputy Clerk or Notary Public
State of Florida
My commission expires:

COUNTY COURT,_____ COUNTY, FLORIDA
SMALL CLAIMS DIVISION
CASE NO._____

_____
_____
PLAINTIFF(S)
Address:

VS.

_____
_____
DEFENDANT(S)
Address:

DEFENDANT'S MOTION FOR CONTINUANCE

Comes now _____
Defendant(s), in the above-styled cause, and respectfully requests that this Honorable Court
reschedule the _____ hearing which is scheduled for the
_____ day of _____, _____. Defendant(s) are unable to appear because
_____
_____
_____
_____

WHEREFORE, Defendant(s) move(s) this Honorable Court for an Order rescheduling the
hearing.

_____
Defendant(s) Signature

_____
_____
Defendant(s) Address

_____
Telephone No: _____

NOTICE OF HEARING

You are hereby notified that a Hearing on the above Motion has been set before Judge
_____, in Room No. ___, _____,
Florida, at _____o'clock _____AM/PM on the _____ day of _____, _____.

I CERTIFY that a copy hereof has been mailed/hand delivered to
_____ this_____ day of _____, _____.

_____
Defendant(s) Signature

COUNTY COURT,_____ COUNTY, FLORIDA
SMALL CLAIMS DIVISION
CASE NO._____

_____
_____
PLAINTIFF(S)
Address:

VS.

_____
_____
DEFENDANT(S)
Address:

MOTION TO SET ASIDE DEFAULT AND DEFAULT JUDGMENT

Comes now _____
Defendant(s), in the above-styled cause, and respectfully requests that this Honorable Court set aside the Default and Default Judgement entered in this cause on the _____ day of _____, _____.

I/We did not appear because: (Give Reason)
_____
_____

and as grounds for a legal defense to this action show the following: (Explain why you are not responsible for claim)
_____
_____
_____

WHEREFORE, Defendant(s) move(s) this Honorable Court for an Order setting aside the Default and Default Judgement previously entered.

_____
Defendant(s) Signature

_____
_____
Defendant(s) Address

_____
Telephone No: _____

NOTICE OF HEARING

You are hereby notified that a Hearing on the above Motion has been set before Judge _____, in Room No. ___, _____, Florida, at ____o'clock _____AM/PM on the _____ day of _____, _____.

I CERTIFY that a copy hereof has been mailed/hand delivered to _____ this_____ day of _____, _____.

_____
Defendant(s) Signature

form 32

COUNTY COURT,_____ **COUNTY, FLORIDA**
SMALL CLAIMS DIVISION
CASE NO._____

_____
_____
PLAINTIFF(S)
Address:

VS.

_____
_____
DEFENDANT(S)
Address:

<u>MOTION FOR RECORDATION OF JUDGMENT AS LIEN</u>

TO THE CLERK OF THE ABOVE STYLED COURT:

    The undersigned hereby requests the Clerk of the above-styled Court to Re-Record the Judgement entered on _____, Book _____ Page _____ in the above styled cause as a Judgement Lien and return a Certified Copy of the same to the address shown below.

_____
Signature of Party Requesting Lien

_____
Address

_____

_____

_____
Phone

CERTIFIED COPY DELIVERED
TO RECORDING

DATE: _____
BY: _____

COUNTY COURT,_____ **COUNTY, FLORIDA**
SMALL CLAIMS DIVISION
CASE NO._____

_____
_____
PLAINTIFF(S)

VS.

_____
_____
DEFENDANT(S)
and

_____
_____
GARNISHEE

MOTION FOR GARNISHMENT
(After Judgment)

On the _____ day of _____, _____, the Plaintiff(s) herein obtained a judgment against the Defendant(s), _____ for the sum of _____ Dollars ($_____) in County Court, _____County, Florida, Small Claims Division; and there remains due and unpaid on said judgment the sum of $_____ plus interest and costs of this proceeding, and the Plaintiff(s) expect(s) to recover said last stated sum, plus interest and costs of this proceeding, in this suit of Garnishment, and do(es) not believe that the said Defendant(s) in said judgment has/have in his/her/their possession visible property upon which a levy can be made sufficiently to satisfy the said judgment, and the Plaintiff(s) move(s) for a Writ of Garnishment to be issued against _____ _____ who Plaintiff(s) has/have reason to believe, has/have in his/her/their hand, possession or control of goods, moneys, chattels or effects belonging to Defendant(s) and that the money or other thing held by the Garnishee subject to the commands of the Writ is not due for the personal labor or services of the head of a family residing in this State.

_____
Plaintiff/Attorney
Address:

Telephone:

COUNTY COURT,_____ COUNTY, FLORIDA
SMALL CLAIMS DIVISION
CASE NO._____

_____
_____

PLAINTIFF(S)

VS.

_____
_____

DEFENDANT(S)
and

_____
_____

GARNISHEE

MOTION FOR CONTINUING WRIT OF GARNISHMENT
Salary or Wages - (after Judgment)

Plaintiff moves the Court for issuance of a Continuing Writ of Garnishment and as grounds states:

On the _____ day of _____, _____, AD, Plaintiff(s) obtained a Judgment against

_____
_____

for the sum of _____ Dollars. ($ _____), in the County Court, _____ County, Florida, Small Claims Division; and there remains due and unpaid on said Judgment the sum of $_____, plus interest and costs, and Plaintiff(s) expect(s) to recover said last stated sum, plus interest and costs of this proceeding, in this suit of Garnishment, and do ____ not believe that the Defendant(s) in said Judgement ha____ in _____ possession visible property upon which a levy can be made sufficiently to satisfy the said Judgment, and the Plaintiff(s) move(s) for a Continuing Writ of Garnishment to be issued pursuant to Florida Statutes, Section 77.0305, against Garnishee _____

_____

who Plaintiff(s) ha____ reason to believe, has in its hands, possession, or control, monies consisting of salary or wages owed and paid periodically to the Defendant(s) _____
_____.

        WHEREFORE, Plaintiff moves the Court to issue a Continuing Writ of Garnishment pursuant to the provisions of Florida Statutes, Section 77.0305.

I certify the Clerks' fees authorized by Chapter 28 and the Court Registry deposit required by Florida Statutes, Section 77.28, have been paid in the amount of $_____ on this _____ day of _____, _____.

_____
Plaintiff

_____
Address

_____

COUNTY COURT,_____ **COUNTY, FLORIDA**
SMALL CLAIMS DIVISION
CASE NO._____

_____
_____
PLAINTIFF(S)

VS.

_____
_____
DEFENDANT(S)

and

_____
_____
GARNISHEE

NOTICE TO DEFENDANT

TO:

NOTICE is hereby given that a writ of garnishment has been issued in the above-captioned case, and that defendant's property in the possession of _____ has been garnisheed, and that, unless defendant, or any person interested in such property, appears before this court, and moves to dissolve said writ on or before _____, _____ judgment by default will be entered.

If the defendant or other recipient of this notice has exemption from garnishment, then such exemption must be asserted as a defense.

CERTIFICATE OF SERVICE

I HEREBY CERTIFY that a copy of the foregoing Notice to Defendant has been furnished by U. S. Mail/Hand delivery to Defendant(s) this _____ day of _____ _____.

_____

IN THE CIRCUIT/COUNTY COURT _____ **COUNTY, FLORIDA**
CIVIL DIVISION

NOTICE TO DEFENDANT OF RIGHT AGAINST GARNISHMENT OF WAGES, MONEY, AND OTHER PROPERTY PURSUANT TO F.S. 77.041

The writ of Garnishment delivered to you with this Notice means that wages, money, and other property belonging to you have been garnished to pay a court judgment against you. HOWEVER, YOU MAY BE ABLE TO KEEP OR RECOVER YOUR WAGES, MONEY, OR PROPERTY. **READ THIS NOTICE CAREFULLY**.

State and Federal laws provide that certain wages, money, and property, even if deposited in the bank, savings and loan, or credit union, may not be taken to pay certain types of court judgments. Such wages, money, and property are exempt from garnishment. The major exemptions are listed below on the form for Claim of Exemption and Request for Hearing. This list does not include all possible exemptions. You should consult a lawyer for specific advice.

TO KEEP YOUR WAGES, MONEY, AND OTHER PROPERTY FROM BEING GARNISHED, OR TO GET BACK ANYTHING ALREADY TAKEN, YOU MUST COMPLETE A FORM FOR CLAIM OF EXEMPTION AND REQUEST FOR HEARING AS SET FORTH BELOW AND HAVE THE FORM NOTARIZED. YOU MUST FILE THE FORM WITH THE CLERK'S OFFICE WITHIN 20 DAYS AFTER THE DATE YOU RECEIVE THIS NOTICE OR YOU MAY LOSE IMPORTANT RIGHTS. YOU MUST ALSO MAIL OR DELIVER A COPY OF THIS FORM TO THE PLAINTIFF AND THE GARNISHEE AT THE ADDRESSES LISTED ON THE WRIT OF GARNISHMENT.

If you request a hearing, it will be held as soon as possible after your request is received by the court. The plaintiff must file an objection within 2 business days if you hand deliver to the plaintiff a copy of the form for Claim of Exemption and Request for Hearing or, alternatively, 7 days if you mailed a copy of the form for claim and request to the plaintiff. If the plaintiff files an objection to your Claim of Exemption and Request for Hearing, the clerk will notify you and the other parties of the time and the date of the hearing. You may attend the hearing with or without an attorney. **If the plaintiff fails to file an objection, no hearing is required, the writ of garnishment will be dissolved and your wages, money, or property will be released.**

YOU MUST FILE THE FORM FOR CLAIM OF EXEMPTION IMMEDIATELY TO KEEP YOUR WAGES, MONEY, OR PROPERTY FROM BEING APPLIED TO THE COURT JUDGMENT. THE CLERK CANNOT GIVE YOU LEGAL ADVICE. IF YOU NEED LEGAL ASSISTANCE YOU SHOULD SEE A LAWYER. IF YOU CANNOT AFFORD A PRIVATE LAWYER, LEGAL SERVICES MAY BE AVAILABLE. CONTACT YOUR LOCAL BAR ASSOCIATION OR ASK THE CLERKS OFFICE ABOUT ANY LEGAL SERVICES PROGRAM IN YOUR AREA.

Karleen F. De Blaker
Clerk of the Circuit Court
Pinellas County

CTCIV229/COCIV76 (6/25/01)   fd4/D15/CrtAdmin/6/25/01

COUNTY COURT,_____ **COUNTY, FLORIDA**
SMALL CLAIMS DIVISION
CASE NO._____

_____
_____
PLAINTIFF(S)

VS.

_____
_____
DEFENDANT(S)
and

_____
_____
GARNISHEE

ACCEPTANCE OF GARNISHMENT
AND MOTION FOR FINAL JUDGMENT

COMES NOW the Plaintiff and accepts the answer of the garnishee _____
_____ filed in this action and moves the Court to enter judgment in accordance with said answer.

CERTIFICATE OF SERVICE

I HEREBY CERTIFY that a copy of the foregoing Notice to Defendant has been furnished by U. S. Mail/Hand delivery to Defendant(s) and the Garnishee this _____ day of _____, _____.

_____

COUNTY COURT,_____ **COUNTY, FLORIDA**
SMALL CLAIMS DIVISION
CASE NO._____

_____
_____
PLAINTIFF(S)

VS.

_____
_____
DEFENDANT(S)
and

_____
_____
GARNISHEE

FINAL JUDGMENT APPROVING GARNISHMENT

THIS CAUSE having come before the Court on the Plaintiff's Acceptance of Garnishment and motion for Final Judgment, and the Court finding that the garnishee, _____, is indebted to the Defendant, _____, and that the Garnishee is entitled to an attorney fee of $_____, it is

ORDERED AND ADJUDGED that the Plaintiff, _____, shall recover the sum of $_____ from the indebted Garnishee; that the Garnishee shall recover $_____ as attorney's fee from the Plaintiff's deposit, for which sums let execution issue forthwith; and that Plaintiff's costs in the amount of $_____ be taxed against Defendant.

DONE AND ORDERED in chambers in _____, _____ County, Florida this ____ day of _____, _____.

_____
County Judge

Copies to:

COUNTY COURT,_____ **COUNTY, FLORIDA**
SMALL CLAIMS DIVISION
CASE NO._____

_____
_____
PLAINTIFF(S)
Address:

VS.

_____
_____
DEFENDANT(S)
Address:

EX PARTE MOTION FOR HEARING IN AID OF EXECUTION

COMES NOW the Judgment Creditor _____ pursuant to Florida Small Claims Rule 7.221, and moves the Court to enter an order requiring the judgment debtor(s) _____, _____, to appear at a hearing in aid of execution for the purpose of examining the judgment debtor(s) regarding his/her/its/their ability to satisfy the final judgment entered in this cause and requiring the judgment debtor(s) to complete a FACT INFORMATION SHEET and bring it to the Hearing in aid of execution.

_____
Judgment Creditor

ORDER FOR HEARING IN AID OF EXECUTION

IT IS ORDERED AND ADJUDGED that the Judgment Debtor(s) _____
_____ shall:

1. Appear before Judge _____ on the _____ day of _____, _____ at _____ o'clock __.m. in Courtroom _____, located at: _____,
Florida to be examined as to the judgment debtor('s)(s') ability to satisfy the final judgment entered in this cause.

2. Bring to the hearing all documents and papers which relate to the Judgment Debtor(s) financial condition and the completed, notarized, fact sheet attached hereto.

Judgment Debtor(s) failure to comply with this Order shall be grounds for contempt.
DONE and ORDERED at _____, _____ County, Florida, this _____ day of _____, _____.

_____
COUNTY COURT JUDGE

Form 7.342

COUNTY COURT,_____ COUNTY, FLORIDA
SMALL CLAIMS DIVISION
CASE NO._____

FACT INFORMATION SHEET

_____
_____
PLAINTIFF(S)

VS.

_____
_____
DEFENDANT(S)

Full Legal Name: _____Residence Address: _____

Nicknames or aliases:_____ Mailing Address (if different):_____

Telephone Numbers:(Home)_____(Business)_____Name of Employer: _____

Address of Employer:_____Position of Job

Description:_____

Rate of Pay: $_____ per_____ Average paycheck $_____ per _____

Average Commissions or Bonuses: $_____ per_____ Commissions or Bonuses are based on_____

Other personal income: $_____from _____

(Explain details on the back of this sheet or an additional sheet if necessary.)

Social Security Number: _____ Birthdate: _____Driver's License Number:_____

Marital Status: _____Spouse's Name: _____

Spouse's Address (if different): _____Spouse's Social Security Number_____

Birthdate: _____Spouse's Employer:_____

Spouse's Average Paycheck or Income: $_____ per _____

Other Family income: $_____ per _____ (Explain details on back of this sheet or an additional sheet if necessary.)

Names and Ages of All Your Children (and addresses if not living with you):_____

_____

Child Support or Alimony Paid: $_____ per _____ Names of Others You Live With: _____

Who is Head of Your Household?_____You _____ Spouse _____ Other Person

Checking Account at: _____ Account #_____Savings Account at: _____ Account #_____

(Describe all other accounts or investments you may have, including stocks, mutual funds, savings bonds, or annuities, on the back of this sheet or an additional sheet if necessary.)

For Real Estate (land) You Own or Are Buying:_____

Address:_____

_____

All Names on Title:_____

Mortgage Owed to:_____ Balanced Owed:_____Monthly Payment: $_____

(Attach a copy of the deed or mortgage, or list the legal description of the property on the back of this sheet or an additional sheet if necessary. Also provide the same information on any other property you own or are buying.)

For All Motor Vehicles You Own or Are Buying:

Year/Make/Model: _____ Color:_____Vehicle ID# _____ Tag No.: _____

Mileage: _____ Loan Owed to: _____Balance on Loan: $_____

Monthly Payment: $_____ (List all other automobiles, as well as other vehicles, such as boats, motorcycles, bicycles, or aircraft, on the back of this sheet or an additional sheet if necessary.)

Have you given, sold, loaned, or transferred any real or personal property worth more than $100 to any person in the last year? If your answer is "yes," describe the property and sale price, and give the name and address of the person who received the property.

Does anyone owe you money? Amount owed: $_____

Name and Address of Person Owing Money:_____

_____

Reason money is owed:_____

_____

Please attach copies of the following:

    a.   Your last pay stub.

    b.   Your last 3 statements for each bank, savings, credit union, or other financial account.

    c.   Your motor vehicle registrations and titles.

    d.   Any deeds or titles to any real estate or personal property you own or are buying, or leases to property you are renting.

UNDER PENALTY OF PERJURY, I SWEAR OR AFFIRM THAT THE FOREGOING ANSWERS ARE TRUE AND COMPLETE.

_____
Judgment Debtor

STATE OF FLORIDA

COUNTY OF _____

    The foregoing instrument was acknowledged before me this _____ day of _____, _____ by _____ who is personally known to me or produced _____ as identification and who _____ did/did____not take an oath.

    WITNESS my hand and official seal, this _____ day of _____, _____.

_____
Notary Public
State of Florida
My commission expires _____

MAIL OR DELIVER A COPY OF THIS FORM TO THE CLERK OF THE COURT, AND MAIL OR DELIVER A COPY OF THE COMPLETED FORM TO THE JUDGMENT CREDITOR OR THE CREDITOR'S ATTORNEY.

form 40

COUNTY COURT,_____ COUNTY, FLORIDA
SMALL CLAIMS DIVISION
CASE NO._____

_____
_____
PLAINTIFF(S)
Address:

VS.

_____
_____
DEFENDANT(S)
Address:

NOTICE OF VOLUNTARY DISMISSAL

Plaintiff(s) _____
in the above styled cause hereby submit this Notice of Voluntary Dismissal as this cause has
been settled between the parties.

CERTIFICATE OF SERVICE

I HEREBY CERTIFY that a copy of the foregoing Notice of Voluntary Dismissal has
been furnished by U. S. Mail/Hand delivery to Defendant(s) this _____ day of
_____, _____.

_____
Signature of Plaintiff

SC 98

148

COUNTY COURT,_____ COUNTY, FLORIDA
SMALL CLAIMS DIVISION
CASE NO._____

_____
_____
PLAINTIFF(S)

Address:

VS.

_____
_____
DEFENDANT(S)

Address:

SATISFACTION OF JUDGMENT

Plaintiff(s) _____, holders of a judgment in the above-styled cause, which judgment was rendered on _____, _____ against _____in the amount of _____ dollars ($_____), and recorded in Official Records Book _____ Page _____, Public Records of _____ County, Florida, hereby acknowledge full payment and satisfaction of said judgment, and hereby consent that said judgment shall be satisfied of record.

_____

_____

Sworn to and subscribed before me by _____ who is personally known to me or produced _____ as identification this_____day of _____, _____.

_____
Notary Public
State of Florida
My commission expires _____

COUNTY COURT,_____ COUNTY, FLORIDA
SMALL CLAIMS DIVISION
CASE NO._____

_____

_____
PLAINTIFF(S)
Address:

VS.

_____

_____
DEFENDANT(S)
Address:

NOTICE OF APPEAL

NOTICE IS HEREBY GIVEN that _____
_____Appellant, appeals to the Circuit Court, _____ Judicial Circuit, Appellate Division, the order of this court rendered _____, _____. [Conformed copies of orders designated in the notice of appeal shall be attached in accordance with rules 9.110(d), and 9.160(c)]. The nature of the order is a Final Judgment.

CERTIFICATE OF SERVICE

I HEREBY CERTIFY that a copy of the foregoing Notice of Voluntary Dismissal has been furnished by U. S. Mail/Hand delivery to Defendant(s) this _____ day of _____, _____.

_____
Signature of Plaintiff

COUNTY COURT,_____ **COUNTY, FLORIDA**
SMALL CLAIMS DIVISION
CASE NO._____

_____

_____
PLAINTIFF(S)

Address:

VS.

_____

_____
DEFENDANT(S)

Address:

NOTICE OF CROSS-APPEAL

NOTICE IS HEREBY GIVEN that _____
_____Appellant, appeals to the Circuit Court, _____ Judicial Circuit, Appellate Division, the order of this court rendered _____, _____. [Conformed copies of orders designated in the notice of appeal shall be attached in accordance with rules 9.110(d), and 9.160(c)]. The nature of the order is a Final Judgment.

CERTIFICATE OF SERVICE

I HEREBY CERTIFY that a copy of the foregoing Notice of Voluntary Dismissal has been furnished by U. S. Mail/Hand delivery to Defendant(s) this _____ day of _____, _____.

_____
Signature of Plaintiff

COUNTY COURT,_____ **COUNTY, FLORIDA**
SMALL CLAIMS DIVISION
CASE NO._____

_____
_____
PLAINTIFF(S)
Address:

VS.

_____
_____
DEFENDANT(S)
Address:

AUTHORIZATION TO REPRESENT CORPORATION

Pursuant to rule 7.050(a)(2), Florida Small Claims Rules, _____
_____ (name of corporation) authorizes its employee,
_____ (name of employee) to represent the corporation in the
above-referenced action.

_____
Officer of the corporation

STATE OF FLORIDA
COUNTY OF_____

    Sworn to and subscribed before me by _____ who is
personally known to me or produced _____ as identification
this_____day of_____, _____.

_____
Deputy Clerk or Notary Public
State of Florida
My commission expires:

FORM B10 (Official Form 10) (4/01)

UNITED STATES BANKRUPTCY COURT _____ DISTRICT OF _____	PROOF OF CLAIM

Name of Debtor	Case Number

NOTE: This form should not be used to make a claim for an administrative expense arising after the commencement of the case. A "request" for payment of an administrative expense may be filed pursuant to 11 U.S.C. § 503.

Name of Creditor (The person or other entity to whom the debtor owes money or property):

☐ Check box if you are aware that anyone else has filed a proof of claim relating to your claim. Attach copy of statement giving particulars.

Name and address where notices should be sent:

☐ Check box if you have never received any notices from the bankruptcy court in this case.

☐ Check box if the address differs from the address on the envelope sent to you by the court.

Telephone number:

THIS SPACE IS FOR COURT USE ONLY

Account or other number by which creditor identifies debtor:

Check here if this claim ☐ replaces / ☐ amends a previously filed claim, dated:_____

1. Basis for Claim

☐ Goods sold
☐ Services performed
☐ Money loaned
☐ Personal injury/wrongful death
☐ Taxes
☐ Other _____

☐ Retiree benefits as defined in 11 U.S.C. § 1114(a)
☐ Wages, salaries, and compensation (fill out below)

Your SS #: _____ _____ _____

Unpaid compensation for services performed

from _____ to_____
     (date)   (date)

2. Date debt was incurred:

3. If court judgment, date obtained:

4. Total Amount of Claim at Time Case Filed: $ _____

If all or part of your claim is secured or entitled to priority, also complete Item 5 or 6 below.

☐ Check this box if claim includes interest or other charges in addition to the principal amount of the claim. Attach itemized statement of all interest or additional charges.

5. Secured Claim.

☐ Check this box if your claim is secured by collateral (including a right of setoff).

Brief Description of Collateral:

☐ Real Estate   ☐ Motor Vehicle
     ☐ Other_____

Value of Collateral: $_____

Amount of arrearage and other charges at time case filed included in secured claim, if any: $_____

6. Unsecured Priority Claim.

☐ Check this box if you have an unsecured priority claim

Amount entitled to priority $_____
Specify the priority of the claim:

☐ Wages, salaries, or commissions (up to $4,650),* earned within 90 days before filing of the bankruptcy petition or cessation of the debtor's business, whichever is earlier - 11 U.S.C. § 507(a)(3).

☐ Contributions to an employee benefit plan - 11 U.S.C. § 507(a)(4).

☐ Up to $2,100* of deposits toward purchase, lease, or rental of property or services for personal, family, or household use - 11 U.S.C. § 507(a)(6).

☐ Alimony, maintenance, or support owed to a spouse, former spouse, or child - 11 U.S.C. § 507(a)(7).

☐ Taxes or penalties owed to governmental units - 11 U.S.C. § 507(a)(8).

☐ Other - Specify applicable paragraph of 11 U.S.C. § 507(a)(____).

*Amounts are subject to adjustment on 4/1/04 and every 3 years thereafter with respect to cases commenced on or after the date of adjustment.

7. Credits: The amount of all payments on this claim has been credited and deducted for the purpose of making this proof of claim.

8. Supporting Documents: *Attach copies of supporting documents,* such as promissory notes, purchase orders, invoices, itemized statements of running accounts, contracts, court judgments, mortgages, security agreements, and evidence of perfection of lien. DO NOT SEND ORIGINAL DOCUMENTS. If the documents are not available, explain. If the documents are voluminous, attach a summary.

9. Date-Stamped Copy: To receive an acknowledgment of the filing of your claim, enclose a stamped, self-addressed envelope and copy of this proof of claim.

THIS SPACE IS FOR COURT USE ONLY

Date	Sign and print the name and title, if any, of the creditor or other person authorized to file this claim (attach copy of power of attorney, if any):

Penalty for presenting fraudulent claim: Fine of up to $500,000 or imprisonment for up to 5 years, or both. 18 U.S.C. §§ 152 and 3571.

INSTRUCTIONS FOR PROOF OF CLAIM FORM

The instructions and definitions below are general explanations of the law. In particular types of cases or circumstances, such as bankruptcy cases that are not filed voluntarily by a debtor, there may be exceptions to these general rules.

—— DEFINITIONS ——

Debtor

The person, corporation, or other entity that has filed a bankruptcy case is called the debtor.

Creditor

A creditor is any person, corporation, or other entity to whom the debtor owed a debt on the date that the bankruptcy case was filed.

Proof of Claim

A form telling the bankruptcy court how much the debtor owed a creditor at the time the bankruptcy case was filed (the amount of the creditor's claim). This form must be filed with the clerk of the bankruptcy court where the bankruptcy case was filed.

Secured Claim

A claim is a secured claim to the extent that the creditor has a lien on property of the debtor (collateral) that gives the creditor the right to be paid from that property before creditors who do not have liens on the property.

Examples of liens are a mortgage on real estate and a security interest in a car, truck, boat, television set, or other item of property. A lien may have been obtained through a court proceeding before the bankruptcy case began; in some states a court judgment is a lien. In addition, to the extent a creditor also owes money to the debtor (has a right of setoff), the creditor's claim may be a secured claim. (See also *Unsecured Claim*.)

Unsecured Claim

If a claim is not a secured claim it is an unsecured claim. A claim may be partly secured and partly unsecured if the property on which a creditor has a lien is not worth enough to pay the creditor in full.

Unsecured Priority Claim

Certain types of unsecured claims are given priority, so they are to be paid in bankruptcy cases before most other unsecured claims (if there is sufficient money or property available to pay these claims). The most common types of priority claims are listed on the proof of claim form. Unsecured claims that are not specifically given priority status by the bankruptcy laws are classified as *Unsecured Nonpriority Claims*.

Items to be completed in Proof of Claim form (if not already filled in)

Court, Name of Debtor, and Case Number:

Fill in the name of the federal judicial district where the bankruptcy case was filed (for example, Central District of California), the name of the debtor in the bankruptcy case, and the bankruptcy case number. If you received a notice of the case from the court, all of this information is near the top of the notice.

Information about Creditor:

Complete the section giving the name, address, and telephone number of the creditor to whom the debtor owes money or property, and the debtor's account number, if any. If anyone else has already filed a proof of claim relating to this debt, if you never received notices from the bankruptcy court about this case, if your address differs from that to which the court sent notice, or if this proof of claim replaces or changes a proof of claim that was already filed, check the appropriate box on the form.

1. Basis for Claim:

Check the type of debt for which the proof of claim is being filed. If the type of debt is not listed, check "Other" and briefly describe the type of debt. If you were an employee of the debtor, fill in your social security number and the dates of work for which you were not paid.

2. Date Debt Incurred:

Fill in the date when the debt first was owed by the debtor.

3. Court Judgments:

If you have a court judgment for this debt, state the date the court entered the judgment.

4. Total Amount of Claim at Time Case Filed:

Fill in the total amount of the entire claim. If interest or other charges in addition to the principal amount of the claim are included, check the appropriate place on the form and attach an itemization of the interest and charges.

5. Secured Claim:

Check the appropriate place if the claim is a secured claim. You must state the type and value of property that is collateral for the claim, attach copies of the documentation of your lien, and state the amount past due on the claim as of the date the bankruptcy case was filed. A claim may be partly secured and partly unsecured. (See DEFINITIONS, above).

6. Unsecured Priority Claim:

Check the appropriate place if you have an unsecured priority claim, and state the amount entitled to priority. (See DEFINITIONS, above). A claim may be partly priority and partly nonpriority if, for example, the claim is for more than the amount given priority by the law. Check the appropriate place to specify the type of priority claim.

7. Credits:

By signing this proof of claim, you are stating under oath that in calculating the amount of your claim you have given the debtor credit for all payments received from the debtor.

8. Supporting Documents:

You must attach to this proof of claim form copies of documents that show the debtor owes the debt claimed or, if the documents are too lengthy, a summary of those documents. If documents are not available, you must attach an explanation of why they are not available.

COUNTY COURT,_____ **COUNTY, FLORIDA**
SMALL CLAIMS DIVISION
CASE NO._____

_____
_____
PLAINTIFF(S)

VS.

_____
_____
DEFENDANT(S)

FINAL JUDGMENT AGAINST _____

It is adjudged that the plaintiff(s), _____
_____, recover from the defendant(s), _____
_____ the sum of $_____ on principal, $_____ as pre-judgment interest, $_____ for attorney fees, with costs of $_____ all of which shall bear interest at the rate of _____% for the current year and thereafter at the pre-vailing rate per year as provided by Florida Statute, for all of which let execution issue.

It is further ordered and adjudged that the defendant(s) shall complete Florida Small Claims Rules Form 7.343 (Fact Information Sheet) and return it to the plaintiff's attorney or to the plaintiff if the plaintiff is not represented by an attorney, within 45 days from the date of this final judgment, unless the final judgment is satisfied or a motion for new trial or notice of appeal is filed.

Jurisdiction of this case is retained to enter further orders that are proper to compel the defendant(s) to complete form 7.343 and return it to the plaintiff's attorney or to the plaintiff if the plaintiff is not represented by an attorney.

ORDERED at _____, Florida, on _____,_____

_____
County Court Judge

Copies furnished to:
PLAINTIFF(S)
DEFENDANT(S)

Plaintiff(s)'s address:

_____
_____

Defendant(s)'s last known address and
Social security Number (if known):

_____
_____
_____

INDEX

legal theory, 9, 29
lemon law, 31
levy, 72
liability, 9, 10, 26, 30, 31, 67
license, 44
lien, 12, 16, 19, 70, 72
limit, 2, 7
limitations of actions, 42

M

malpractice, 13, 30-31, 42
mediation, 13, 46
minors, 16, 17, 40
mistake, 42
motion for continuance, 54
motion for new trial, 79
motion for rehearing, 79
motion for writ of garnishment, 73
multiple parties, 16
mutually mistaken, 21

N

negligence, 9, 27, 29, 30
negotiation, 13, 21
new trial, 79
nolo contendere, 27
notice, 73
notice of appeal, 78
notice to defendant, 73

O

open account, 23-24
opening statement, 54
oral agreement, 64

P

parent, 16
parol evidence rule, 65
partnerships, 18
    limited, 18
perjury, 20
personal property. *See property*
piercing the corporate veil, 17
plaintiff, 36, 37, 42, 45, 46, 47, 48, 49, 54, 59, 67, 70, 71
preponderance of the evidence, 65
presentation of case, 56-58
pretrial conference, 3, 6, 51-52, 63, 77, 78
process server, 33
promissory note, 13, 19, 25, 35, 39, 45
proof, 11, 65

proof of claim, 75
property, 1, 10, 16, 19, 22, 30, 67, 68, 69, 70, 72, 73, 74, 75
    exempt, 69-70
    personal, 22, 69
    real, 70
property records, 12

Q

quantum meruit, 29
questions of fact, 77, 78

R

real estate. *See property*
rebuttal, 54, 56
reform, 21
registered agent, 17
rehearing, 79
remedies, 21
replevin, 19, 22
request for alias or pluries service, 33
res judicata, 38
rescission, 21
restitution, 21
rule of sequestration, 55
rules of evidence, 22
rules of procedure, 55

S

sales, 45
security deposit, 26
services, 23, 24, 43
settlement, 3, 40, 46, 52-53
small claims rule, 4, 5
specific performance, 21
spouse, 16, 69, 70
statement of claim, 3, 22, 32, 36, 37, 48, 55
statute of frauds, 39-40, 64
statute of limitations, 13, 41-42
stipulation, 35, 51, 53, 59
stipulation to stay entry of judgment, 46, 59
subpoena, 6, 62, 63
subpoena duces tecum, 62, 71
suggestion of bankruptcy, 75
summons, 35

T

tenant, 25
testimony, 52, 55
traffic violation, 27
trial, 32, 51, 52, 53, 54-55, 56, 58, 59, 62, 63, 74,
    77, 78
      procedure, 54
trustees, 16

U

Uniform Commercial Code, 45
usury, 43

V

venue, 19, 36
victim, 56

W

waiver, 44
warranty, 28, 29, 31
warranty of fitness for a particular purpose., 29
warranty of merchantability, 29
warranty of title, 28
witnesses, 3, 6, 27, 46, 52, 54, 55, 56, 57, 58, 61,
    62-63, 78
      expert, 6, 63-64
      fees, 63
writ of garnishment, 73

SPHINX® PUBLISHING ORDER FORM

BILL TO:		SHIP TO:	

Phone #	Terms	F.O.B.	Chicago, IL	Ship Date

Charge my: ☐ VISA ☐ MasterCard ☐ American Express

☐ **Money Order or Personal Check**

Credit Card Number   Expiration Date

Qty	ISBN	Title	Retail	Ext.
		SPHINX PUBLISHING NATIONAL TITLES		
	1-57248-148-X	Cómo Hacer su Propio Testamento	$16.95	
	1-57248-147-1	Cómo Solicitar su Propio Divorcio	$24.95	
	1-57248-226-5	Cómo Restablecer su propio Credito y Renegociar sus Deudas	$21.95	
	1-57248-166-8	The Complete Book of Corporate Forms	$24.95	
	1-57248-163-3	Crime Victim's Guide to Justice (2E)	$21.95	
	1-57248-159-5	Essential Guide to Real Estate Contracts	$18.95	
	1-57248-160-9	Essential Guide to Real Estate Leases	$18.95	
	1-57248-139-0	Grandparents' Rights (3E)	$24.95	
	1-57248-188-9	Guía de Inmigración a Estados Unidos (3E)	$24.95	
	1-57248-187-0	Guía de Justicia para Víctimas del Crimen	$21.95	
	1-57248-103-X	Help Your Lawyer Win Your Case (2E)	$14.95	
	1-57248-164-1	How to Buy a Condominium or Townhome (2E)	$19.95	
	1-57248-191-9	How to File Your Own Bankruptcy (5E)	$21.95	
	1-57248-132-3	How to File Your Own Divorce (4E)	$24.95	
	1-57248-100-5	How to Form a DE Corporation from Any State	$24.95	
	1-57248-083-1	How to Form a Limited Liability Company	$22.95	
	1-57248-099-8	How to Form a Nonprofit Corporation	$24.95	
	1-57248-133-1	How to Form Your Own Corporation (3E)	$24.95	
	1-57248-224-9	How to Form Your Own Partnership (2E)	$24.95	
	1-57248-119-6	How to Make Your Own Will (2E)	$16.95	
	1-57248-200-1	How to Register Your Own Copyright (4E)	$24.95	
	1-57248-104-8	How to Register Your Own Trademark (3E)	$21.95	
	1-57071-349-9	How to Win Your Unemployment Compensation Claim	$21.95	
	1-57248-118-8	How to Write Your Own Living Will (2E)	$16.95	
	1-57248-156-0	How to Write Your Own Premarital Agreement (3E)	$24.95	
	1-57248-158-7	Incorporate in Nevada from Any State	$24.95	
	1-57071-333-2	Jurors' Rights (2E)	$12.95	
	1-57071-400-2	Legal Research Made Easy (2E)	$16.95	
	1-57248-165-X	Living Trusts and Other Ways to Avoid Probate (3E)	$24.95	

Qty	ISBN	Title	Retail	Ext.
	1-57248-186-2	Manual de Beneficios para el Seguro Social	$18.95	
	1-57248-220-6	Mastering the MBE	$16.95	
	1-57248-167-6	Most Valuable Bus. Legal Forms You'll Ever Need (3E)	$21.95	
	1-57248-130-7	Most Valuable Personal Legal Forms You'll Ever Need	$24.95	
	1-57248-098-X	The Nanny and Domestic Help Legal Kit	$22.95	
	1-57248-089-0	Neighbor v. Neighbor (2E)	$16.95	
	1-57248-169-2	The Power of Attorney Handbook (4E)	$19.95	
	1-57248-149-8	Repair Your Own Credit and Deal with Debt	$18.95	
	1-57248-168-4	The Social Security Benefits Handbook (3E)	$18.95	
	1-57071-399-5	Unmarried Parents' Rights	$19.95	
	1-57071-354-5	U.S.A. Immigration Guide (3E)	$19.95	
	1-57248-192-7	The Visitation Handbook	$18.95	
	1-57248-138-2	Winning Your Personal Injury Claim (2E)	$24.95	
	1-57248-162-5	Your Right to Child Custody, Visitation and Support (2E)	$24.95	
	1-57248-157-9	Your Rights When You Owe Too Much	$16.95	
		CALIFORNIA TITLES		
	1-57248-150-1	CA Power of Attorney Handbook (2E)	$18.95	
	1-57248-151-X	How to File for Divorce in CA (3E)	$26.95	
	1-57071-356-1	How to Make a CA Will	$16.95	
	1-57248-145-5	How to Probate and Settle an Estate in California	$26.95	
	1-57248-146-3	How to Start a Business in CA	$18.95	
	1-57248-194-3	How to Win in Small Claims Court in CA (2E)	$18.95	
	1-57248-196-X	The Landlord's Legal Guide in CA	$24.95	
		FLORIDA TITLES		
	1-57071-363-4	Florida Power of Attorney Handbook (2E)	$16.95	
	1-57248-176-5	How to File for Divorce in FL (7E)	$26.95	
	1-57248-177-3	How to Form a Corporation in FL (5E)	$24.95	
	1-57248-203-6	How to Form a Limited Liability Co. in FL (2E)	$24.95	
	1-57071-401-0	How to Form a Partnership in FL	$22.95	

Form Continued on Following Page   **SUBTOTAL**

To order, call Sourcebooks at 1-800-432-7444 or FAX (630) 961-2168 (Bookstores, libraries, wholesalers—please call for discount)
Prices are subject to change without notice.
Find more legal information at: www.SphinxLegal.com

SPHINX® PUBLISHING ORDER FORM

Qty	ISBN	Title	Retail	Ext.
	1-57248-113-7	How to Make a FL Will (6E)	$16.95	
	1-57248-088-2	How to Modify Your FL Divorce Judgment (4E)	$24.95	
	1-57248-144-7	How to Probate and Settle an Estate in FL (4E)	$26.95	
	1-57248-081-5	How to Start a Business in FL (5E)	$16.95	
	1-57248-204-4	How to Win in Small Claims Court in FL (7E)	$18.95	
	1-57248-202-8	Land Trusts in Florida (6E)	$29.95	
	1-57248-123-4	Landlords' Rights and Duties in FL (8E)	$21.95	
GEORGIA TITLES				
	1-57248-137-4	How to File for Divorce in GA (4E)	$21.95	
	1-57248-180-3	How to Make a GA Will (4E)	$21.95	
	1-57248-140-4	How to Start a Business in Georgia (2E)	$16.95	
ILLINOIS TITLES				
	1-57071-405-3	How to File for Divorce in IL (2E)	$21.95	
	1-57248-170-6	How to Make an IL Will (3E)	$16.95	
	1-57071-416-9	How to Start a Business in IL (2E)	$18.95	
	1-57248-078-5	Landlords' Rights & Duties in IL	$21.95	
MASSACHUSETTS TITLES				
	1-57248-128-5	How to File for Divorce in MA (3E)	$24.95	
	1-57248-115-3	How to Form a Corporation in MA	$24.95	
	1-57248-108-0	How to Make a MA Will (2E)	$16.95	
	1-57248-106-4	How to Start a Business in MA (2E)	$18.95	
	1-57248-209-5	The Landlord's Legal Guide in MA	$24.95	
MICHIGAN TITLES				
	1-57071-409-6	How to File for Divorce in MI (2E)	$21.95	
	1-57248-182-X	How to Make a MI Will (3E)	$16.95	
	1-57248-183-8	How to Start a Business in MI (3E)	$18.95	
MINNESOTA TITLES				
	1-57248-142-0	How to File for Divorce in MN	$21.95	
	1-57248-179-X	How to Form a Corporation in MN	$24.95	
	1-57248-178-1	How to Make a MN Will (2E)	$16.95	
NEW YORK TITLES				
	1-57248-193-5	Child Custody, Visitation and Support in NY	$26.95	
	1-57248-141-2	How to File for Divorce in NY (2E)	$26.95	
	1-57248-105-6	How to Form a Corporation in NY	$24.95	
	1-57248-095-5	How to Make a NY Will (2E)	$16.95	
	1-57248-199-4	How to Start a Business in NY (2E)	$18.95	

Qty	ISBN	Title	Retail	Ext.
	1-57248-198-6	How to Win in Small Claims Court in NY (2E)	$18.95	
	1-57071-186-0	Landlords' Rights and Duties in NY	$21.95	
	1-57071-188-7	New York Power of Attorney Handbook	$19.95	
	1-57248-122-6	Tenants' Rights in NY	$21.95	
NORTH CAROLINA TITLES				
	1-57248-185-4	How to File for Divorce in NC (3E)	$22.95	
	1-57248-129-3	How to Make a NC Will (3E)	$16.95	
	1-57248-184-6	How to Start a Business in NC (3E)	$18.95	
	1-57248-091-2	Landlords' Rights & Duties in NC	$21.95	
OHIO TITLES				
	1-57248-190-0	How to File for Divorce in OH (2E)	$24.95	
	1-57248-174-9	How to Form a Corporation in OH	$24.95	
	1-57248-173-0	How to Make an OH Will	$16.95	
PENNSYLVANIA TITLES				
	1-57248-211-7	How to File for Divorce in PA (3E)	$26.95	
	1-57248-094-7	How to Make a PA Will (2E)	$16.95	
	1-57248-112-9	How to Start a Business in PA (2E)	$18.95	
	1-57071-179-8	Landlords' Rights and Duties in PA	$19.95	
TEXAS TITLES				
	1-57248-171-4	Child Custody, Visitation, and Support in TX	$22.95	
	1-57248-172-2	How to File for Divorce in TX (3E)	$24.95	
	1-57248-114-5	How to Form a Corporation in TX (2E)	$24.95	
	1-57071-417-7	How to Make a TX Will (2E)	$16.95	
	1-57248-214-1	How to Probate and Settle an Estate in TX (3E)	$26.95	
	1-57248-228-1	How to Start a Business in TX (3E)	$18.95	
	1-57248-111-0	How to Win in Small Claims Court in TX (2E)	$16.95	
	1-57248-110-2	Landlords' Rights and Duties in TX (2E)	$21.95	

SUBTOTAL THIS PAGE _____

SUBTOTAL PREVIOUS PAGE _____

Shipping — $5.00 for 1st book, $1.00 each additional _____

Illinois residents add 6.75% sales tax _____

Connecticut residents add 6.00% sales tax _____

TOTAL _____

To order, call Sourcebooks at 1-800-432-7444 or FAX (630) 961-2168 (Bookstores, libraries, wholesalers—please call for discount)
Prices are subject to change without notice.
Find more legal information at: www.SphinxLegal.com